BRAVER, BOLDER, BETTER

Small Steps to Fire Up Your Brilliance

and Create the Change

You Want to See

RANDA MODJISSOLA ADECHOUBOU

IYA-OLOKA
PUBLISHING.CO

COTONOU JOHANNESBURG PARIS MELBOURNE TOKYO WASHINGTON, D.C

BRAVER, BOLDER, BETTER

This book is not intended to replace the advice of a trained psychological professional. Readers are advised to consult a qualified professional regarding treatment. The author and publisher specifically disclaim liability, loss, or risk, personal or otherwise, which is incurred as a consequence, directly or indirectly, of the use or application of any of the contents of this book.

Published in the United States by Iya-Oloka

bawo@iya-oloka.com

www.iya-oloka.com

Library of Congress Cataloging-in-Publication data is available upon request.
ISBN: 978-1-7352008-3-5

PRINTED IN THE UNITED STATES OF AMERICA
Editing by Grant Murray

Authors, personalities and brands featured in this book are used as examples. These people and brands have not endorsed the book or its advice and suggestions. Nor does the inclusion in this book mean an endorsement of the writer of the featured individuals' tips and strategies.

To my parents Makarimi and Edwige Adechoubou,
I am who I am because of you. Thank you for giving me the
greatest gift I could have wished for by believing in me.

To Koudousse, Ahmed, Nadiath, Yacine, Rockyath
We rise, shine and thrive together and forever.

To you,

You are braver than you know. Bolder than you can imagine and already better than yesterday.

You can do it.

CONTENTS

INTRODUCTION		**1**
YOUR 30-DAY PLAN		**7**
BRAVER		**17**
CHAPTER 1	**Step Up**	**19**
CHAPTER 2	**Know Yourself**	**27**
CHAPTER 3	**Love Yourself**	**37**
CHAPTER 4	**Believe In Yourself**	**45**
CHAPTER 5	**Live Your Truth**	**55**
CHAPTER 6	**The Approval Fix**	**63**
CHAPTER 7	**The Emotion Code**	**73**
CHAPTER 8	**You Be You**	**83**
CHAPTER 9	**Let It Go**	**93**
CHAPTER 10	**Find Your Magic**	**103**
BOLDER		**111**
CHAPTER 11	**Self-Care Matters**	**113**
CHAPTER 12	**Fear Is The Fuel**	**123**
CHAPTER 13	**The Power Of Rituals**	**133**
CHAPTER 14	**The Rules To Break**	**141**
CHAPTER 15	**Rising Strong**	**151**

CHAPTER 16   **Breaking Habits, Making Habits**   **159**

CHAPTER 17   **Getting Things Done**   **169**

CHAPTER 18   **Destination Goal**   **179**

CHAPTER 19   **Finish What You Start**   **189**

CHAPTER 20   **Building Systems For Your Life**   **199**

BETTER   **209**

CHAPTER 21   **Fail Forward**   **211**

CHAPTER 22   **Focus**   **223**

CHAPTER 23   **Find Your Strengths**   **233**

CHAPTER 24   **Find Your Why**   **241**

CHAPTER 25   **Just Listen**   **251**

CHAPTER 26   **You, Inc.**   **259**

CHAPTER 27   **Promote Yourself**   **267**

CHAPTER 28   **Your Network Is Your Net Worth**   **279**

CHAPTER 29   **You 2.0**   **287**

CHAPTER 30   **The Art Of Gratitude**   **295**

EPILOGUE   **304**

What's Next?   *307*

Sharing Is Caring   *308*

Acknowledgments   *309*

Resources   *312*

Notes   *315*

Index   *325*

About The Author   *331*

INTRODUCTION

"Do not fear a life without the presence of those who gave up on you.
Instead, fear a life where you have abandoned yourself."

—DODINSKY

Where am I? Why am I here? Two questions that changed everything for me and could do the same for you.

A few years ago I embarked on a journey that would change my life. At first, the trip showed all the promises of excitement, discovery and joy. I was looking forward to all the potential experiences filled with wonder. But what was supposed to be an exciting and magical ride grew into a rather devastating, realization-filled journey. Halfway through my trip I could barely recognize the stops I was making, the places I was at, the people I had befriended and the values I had adopted.

What did I expect though? I went on a hopeful trip without a clear end-goal in mind. No answer to the questions of "where should I be at?" or "where do I want to find myself in?" So, there I was, as isolated, directionless and dull as that train ride, wondering how I got there in the first place.

Where am I?

I can't tell you exactly how long that journey was, but it was no joy ride. Ultimately, it hit me. As they say, "the truth shall set you free." My

1

truth was this: I had abandoned myself. I had abandoned my dreams and goals, giving everything else precedence over me. I didn't know that the very moment wherein I started saying "yes" when I truly wanted to say "no" marked my path towards this self-destructive pattern of behavior. I didn't know that settling for less than my heart's content would eventually lead to my heart's distress.

I had abandoned myself.

Needless to say, that same disturbing journey was my turning point. I learned that, as poisonously selfless as it was, the darkness of that train ride was necessary for me to realize that I should jump off it sooner rather than later. Without it, I wouldn't have shifted to this new direction. Sure, it was devastating, but it served as a lesson while walking my path towards finding myself.

No matter how deep into the miserable journey we have fallen, it's never too late to leave for our own sake and that of our *own* ambitions. The glory over self-abandonment lies in that first choice: it lies in valuing ourselves over the many people who don't see our worth and only seek to exhaust our vitality. If there's anyone who is in control, it should be us. We are the writers of our own stories.

WHY I WROTE THIS BOOK

The journey to finding oneself is rocky and rather off-putting. I do not have the most definite solutions because I continue to learn about myself day after day. But occasionally life gives you something that resembles the perfect answer, yet when you adopt it, you fall flat on the cold ground. When this misfortune happens a couple of times, there will exist a temptation to give in and give up. Don't. More than anything, we must try to rise up and stand firmly in our power so we can finally walk towards the right path where we can discover what must truly be done, in consideration of all that we are and all that we want to become.

In my quest to redeem myself, I didn't have a fit-for-purpose guide to help me. Don't get me wrong, there was plenty of information available, but I wanted more than mere *instructions* that only ever try to cover deep wounds with a band aid. What I longed for were targeted and practical accounts so I wouldn't have to decode the book. The reason why I wrote **Braver, Bolder, Better** is because I felt the urge to give the rest of the "abandoned" a push into the right direction by giving them a realistic account of my battles as opposed to a deceptive tale of hope. After all, we might be people of different worlds but we come with a single, intense desire to be our most authentic selves, to be and give our best.

After getting off that wholly devastating, directionless train ride, I made it a point to channel my newly acquired awareness into something that would give me a greater sense of purpose. And so, I crowd-funded the resources necessary to write the "hidden answers" which I hoped to find for so long but couldn't. Toni Morrison said it best, "If you find a book you really want to read but it hasn't been written yet, then you must write it." So I did, and here we are.

In **Braver, Bolder, Better** my hope is to set you free from being reactive and inspire you to be proactive. The choice still lies with you, whether or not you take up my challenges. However, I won't stop from illuminating your path so that you can vividly step beyond your comfort zone and face the lurking monsters in your head that taunt you into self-abandonment.

To ensure that you won't be alone in this life-changing progression, I will also share my learnings from people who had the same experiences as I did yet took the leap to embrace the very principles outlined in this book. These people also include experts who have managed to find their way into self-actualization and have used their acquired knowledge to teach us how to enhance our daily experiences. With all of this wisdom at your disposal, you'll be able to re-claim your most authentic self.

Braver, Bolder, Better is more than a cute title I pieced together. Instead, it's a friendly invitation to begin weaving your own story—personal choices and all. It will take ounces of *bravery* to face your fears and break loose from all that had been holding you back. It will take tons of *boldness* to make the toughest of choices once you're finally given the most coherent answers. It will take constant *betterment* of self, both physically and mentally, to not let opportunities pass and to achieve the greatest outward expression necessary for victory. With these three combined together and blended with practical insights on top of greatly empowering exercises, you will be able to tap into your own power and attain the self-compassion that is key to undoing years of forgetting your essence.

If you seek to transform and cultivate your highest potential, perhaps it's time to *choose* to act. But hey, you're off to a great start! Congratulations on your first, extremely effective decision: picking up this book and allowing yourself to be immersed into its awakening capacity!

Cheers to a Braver, Bolder, Better you!

HOW TO USE THIS BOOK

Every chapter in this book is designed in a way that builds on the previous one. Even though I suggest you read the book in sequence, it's possible that some parts may speak to you more than others. That's totally fine! How you go about working your way through the chapters is up to you, but don't forget to go back and read the chapters you've skipped over.

While you might be tempted to dismiss some of the exercises as easy and not worth attempting, I strongly suggest that you don't do so. Each exercise was chosen specifically to assist you in forming healthy habits to align with your authentic self. If you skip one, chances are you'll ignore the rest as you go.

The most important thing is to put your learnings into action—doing something yields better results than blindly following.

Each chapter in **Braver, Bolder, Better** starts off with an introduction to a specific topic, followed by an expert's advice or story. It's important to read through these so that you'll be able to remember passages that speak to you, maybe even highlighting a statement or two. After that, we'll proceed to the daily exercises—give them your best shot!

YOUR 30-DAY PLAN

—

Think of this book as a conversation with a friend during a road trip. Whenever I catch up with a friend I haven't seen in a while, we begin by talking about where we are at that given point in time: what have we done so far, and what has stopped us from going further. We compare our current states with all our plans and proceed with debates on what we should change—what mindsets and actions should we employ if we wanted to be where we're initially set out.

This is exactly what you should expect here as well.

During this Braver, Bolder, Better road trip, you will spend 30 days in the driver's seat, clearly seeing the landscapes and obstacles. In this month-long action-packed adventure, you will embark on a path to find the tools that will help you eradicate the limitations that have long held you back. You'll also acquire new skills and learn new strategies to create the blueprint towards a better life.

It's time to activate becoming braver, bolder and better. To do so, each part of your transformation revolves around a unitary theme and split into two weeks that contains five chapters each. Every chapter, every story and every practice are an invitation to shed, learn and move forward. Embrace all the steps and be patient with the more difficult techniques. There's no shortcut to greatness, there's only a confident individual who acknowledges the challenges of life and opts to confront them.

Be prepared for the journey. You'll need a notepad and pen, but more importantly, you'll need commitment and consistency.

Let's get into it.

Here's a little preview of what you're about to encounter in this book. Buckle up, you're in for a wild ride!

BRAVER

It's our first stop on this journey together. We'll start strongly by spending the first two weeks uncovering the behaviors, patterns and thoughts that may be holding you back. As they say, "new wine must be put into fresh wineskins," and that's exactly what we'll be doing here—getting rid of the old and replacing it with something newer, sturdier and healthier.

WEEK 1: MAKE YOUR BED

Day 1: Step Up

To stand firmly on your own two feet, you must acknowledge that no one is going to hand you exactly what you want. If you want to make changes in your life, the best companion would be yourself. Read the story of **Dwayne "The Rock" Johnson** and his seven bucks moment—truly inspirational stuff!

Day 2: Know Yourself

There's nothing more important than being in touch with your true, authentic self. After all, you determine what you want, where you'll go and what you will do to get there. Take a look through **Deepak Chopra's** tips to help you look inward so that you can project a better outward version of yourself.

Day 3: Love Yourself

The relationship you have with yourself determines the relationship you have with others. By embracing your flaws you can radiate positive energy towards everyone else—use **Louise Hay's** unique mirror work philosophy to help you get there.

Day 4: Believe in Yourself

What you think, you become. Despite desiring to go forward, you might find yourself in quicksand due to your harsh and self-criticizing mindset. Find out how **Shad Helmstetter's** hacks using the power of repetition can help you overcome your own negative narrative.

Day 5: Live Your Truth

If you don't know your values, you will end up following someone else's. Values are not merely there for the sake of politeness, they determine the choices you make, your dreams and your way of life. Learn more about **James Clear's** Integrity Report and discover the benefits of establishing your values and living according to them.

WEEK 2: UNSTUCK YOURSELF

Day 6: The Approval Fix

Humans evolved to want to be liked—it's in our DNA to strive for connection and togetherness. But if you find yourself always seeking validation from others and putting your own opinions last, your progress in life will be limited. **Wayne Dyer's** wisdom might just give you the push that you need towards self-acceptance.

Day 7: The Emotion Code

Are you in control of your emotions or is it the other way around? Effective emotional management doesn't involve bottling them up but rather listening to your heart, heartily. The good folks at the **Gottman Institute** have figured out what your emotions might be trying to tell you.

Day 8: You Be You

There's always going to be someone richer, prettier and smarter than you if you keep thinking about yourself in comparison with other people. Why does life have to be a competition? Everyone blooms at different times. The powerful story of **Emily Blunt** and how she overcame her stuttering to become a leading Hollywood actress will show you that your growth relies on no one but yourself.

Day 9: Let It Go

Letting go of all the "what-if" scenarios might be hard to do, but it's the only way forward. Holding grudges will only weigh you down. Freeing yourself from the past is one of the best gifts you can give yourself, as demonstrated by **Everett Worthington's** REACH model.

Day 10: Find Your Magic

The only way to learn how to swim is by jumping in the water. Fear is an instinct, but you can't let it stop you from showing up and stepping out. Discover how **Shonda Rhimes'** year of saying "yes" can motivate you to make braver and bolder choices too.

BOLDER

You've now done the inner work, asked the tough questions and confronted the critic that resides in your mind. But this is not the time to sit back and relax—get ready to lay the foundation for a new chapter. The building materials for the "bolder you" are up next. Let's get into it, shall we?

WEEK 3: MIND YOUR BUSINESS

Day 11: Self-Care Matters

Self-care is essential. Just as you can only grow plants in fertile soil, you can only be your best if you indulge and invest in your development. Think beyond bubble baths, champagne showers and impulsive shopping sprees—what are the ingredients to meaningful self-care? Take a look at our recommendations to spark your creativity in designing your own self-care routine.

Day 12: Fear Is The Fuel

We all have fears, but some decide to entertain them when others choose to conquer them. No matter which camp you belong to, the only way forward is through. Renowned author **Susan Jeffers'** five truths about fears is a must-read if you want liberate yourself from what's holding you back.

Day 13: The Power of Rituals

Did you know that the way you start and end your day can have a significant impact on your productivity and overall wellness? Daily rituals create a ripple effect across your life. Don't believe me? Check out **Benjamin Franklin's** routines and decide for yourself.

Day 14: The Rules to Break

Imagine a world without law and order. Now, do the opposite and think about living in a world where rules were never broken either. What about all the inventions and discoveries you enjoy today? Many people had to go against the grain to make those happen. Your professional and personal life may benefit from a bit of rule-breaking too. Find out how **Madam CJ Walker,** the first female self-made millionaire in America, flipped the rule book to create her long-lasting empire.

Day 15: Rising Strong

Life can sometimes make you feel like you're caught in a labyrinth. Hard times may come your way, but the key is to remember that they won't last forever. The story of professional surfer **Bethany Hamilton** will inspire you to pick yourself up and keep going.

WEEK 4: GOOD TO GREAT

Day 16: Breaking Habits, Making Habits

Like most people, do you struggle to stick to your New Year's resolutions? Forming new habits is an essential skill and lies at the core of long-lasting change. **Dr. BJ Fogg's** groundbreaking tiny habits method will help you break up with your old ways.

Day 17: Getting Things Done

You always seem to have a plan, but you never get anything done. We've all been the spokesperson for "tomorrow is another day" at some point in time. **Mel Robbins'** practical tips might just be what you need to move at full speed in your life without procrastination getting the better of you.

Day 18: Destination Goal

You have to have goals or else you'll be drifting aimlessly through life. How do you set goals? Do you exert your best efforts to achieve them? **David Allen's** framework will help you bridge the gap between dreaming about it and actually doing it.

Day 19: Finish What You Start

Do you have enough discipline to finish this book? Ha, got you! Jokes aside, you won't be able to accomplish much if you don't employ some discipline in your life. **Brian Tracy's** seven-step formula can help you add structure to your day-to-day routine.

Day 20: Building Systems For Your Life

Whether you realize it or not, you currently have an operating system in your life—in other words, your own way of doing things. We all do. But is it effective? Like on a computer, your operating system will dictate how effectively you'll function. Take a look through the simple steps from **Jane Taylor** to optimize your operating system in no time.

BETTER

We have tackled a lot, but our ride is about to get even better! Speaking of better, this is the week to unravel the many different ways to "do better." From developing the grandest vision of your life, to learning how to be more grateful—striving for self-improvement has never looked this good.

WEEK 5: BECOMING

Day 21: Failing Forward

There's no right way or wrong way to fail. You're bound to stumble occasionally and that's okay. How else are you going to learn? Failure can lead to a change of direction that becomes groundbreaking. Read **Jack Ma's** impressive story on how his countless failures eventually led him to a booming success.

Day 22: Focus

What you focus on, grows. That's why you have to be so careful about what you concentrate your attention on. We all have to-do lists and we want to get through everything on them. But what if I told you that there was a better way? Check out **Gary W. Keller** and **Jay Papasan's** advice on being laser-focused and you might just eliminate your distractions for good!

Day 23: Find Your Strengths

Focus on your perfections and not your flaws. But how do you do that, and where do you go to uncover your potential? **Marcus Buckingham** has an interesting take on how to identify your strengths. Get on it!

Day 24: Find Your Why

Vision, North Star, purpose, your why—they are all essentially the same thing. They all center on what you're planning to do with your precious life. Author **Richard Leider's** purpose formula will help you figure it out in style.

Day 25: Just Listen

Are you fully present when listening or is your mind distracted? Most of us fail to listen effectively and crucially miss out on important information, opportunities and memories. Going through **Julian Treasure's** tips will help you tune in better to your next conversations.

WEEK 6: RISING STRONG

Day 26: You, Inc.

If the thought of being a salesperson makes you cringe, you're not alone. Yet all of us are, in fact, salespeople, whether we realize it or not. Life in itself is a sales pitch. You sell yourself on a date, at work, at parties, with your kids. You frequently have to convince others to give you what you want. Use **Dr. Cialdini's** 6 Principles of Persuasion to sell yourself effectively.

Day 27: Promote Yourself

You know the saying, "build it, and they will come"? What happens when no one comes? We apply the same approach to our dreams, goals and careers. We wait for people to sponsor our ideas, but how do they know we're even qualified for it? There's nothing wrong with self-promotion—you've got to be your No.1 fan before the world can join in to cheer you on. **Peggy Klaus'** tips will teach you how to be your own best spokesperson.

Day 28: Your Network Is Your Net worth

Living like Robinson Crusoe on your imaginary island won't get you far. Building a network of allies, supporters and friends is crucial to your growth. Are you ready to build your connections? Consider **Keith Ferrazzi's** incredible tips to help you get started.

Day 29: You 2.0

You're not a wax figure, you know! Life is about dynamics—changing, adding and deleting are necessary steps. If you're no longer satisfied with the way your personal and professional life is panning out, dare to reinvent yourself. From publicist to award-winning film producer, **Ava Duvernay's** story will inspire you to see what's possible beyond the ordinary.

Day 30: The Art of Gratitude

Gratefulness for what you already have will open the doors for more. There are so many gratitude training lessons you could adopt, but the key is to pick the one you'll enjoy the most. **Tim Ferris'** tips on practicing gratitude will inspire you to get going with your own.

BRAVER

//To be stronger in the face of fear

———

It all starts here. It starts now.

The epic journey you are about to embark on demands that you face your deepest fears so that they no longer hold you back.

Overcoming stifling habits requires persistence and commitment. If you're reading this, it means that you're ready to go after what you deserve.

Let's go!

CHAPTER 1

Step Up

—

"The moment you accept responsibility for
everything in your life is the moment you gain
the power to change anything in your life."

—HAL ELROD

I'm not very fond of circus shows.

Never have been, never will be. Even the ones without animals seldom entertain me. I know what you're thinking, "She's scared of clowns." I don't mind them. But at the end of each year, I'm forced to sit in on a circus. One that occurs in the workplace. Yes, that's right, the dreaded annual performance review. And I was to be this show's main act!

If only I could disappear to a far-off land. I'd go to Marrakesh and finally cross it off my bucket list. The mosaic of colors, the bustling souks, the beautiful riads. Oh, and don't forget the unbelievable shopping adventures. I wish. But here I was, sitting in a one-on-one meeting with another performer—my manager. What this performance lacked in jaw-dropping entertainment, it made up for in mind-boggling moments of sheer ridiculousness.

The most crucial one happened just fifteen minutes into my review. While discussing progression and several grievances I've had over the years, my manager casually remarked, "You're the only one responsible for your career."

Wait... what? I started rocking in my chair, trying to feign a semi-coherent witty comeback. I could not think of anything. What exactly did she mean?

This company had been my life for the past few years. I had been giving my EVERYTHING to this place and I expected THEM to be responsible for my career. Yes, them! Isn't a job about give and take? I expected them to invest in my career development and to give me access to training sessions and mentors. I assumed they would help me figure out what to do next. Perhaps, even give me the moon. Is that too much to ask?

With just one sentence my manager threw a banana crème pie straight into my face—and there was no clown around to even make the whole thing funny. As bestselling author and motivational speaker Denis Waitley once said, "There are two primary choices in life: to accept conditions as they exist, or accept the responsibility for changing them." I chose the latter.

That encounter was one of the most defining moments of my career. It woke me up from a state of complacency. It shook me and made me realize that NO ONE was going to have my best interests at heart like I was. No one had taken my power away. I had willingly given it away and I wasn't even laying claim to it anymore. I had to decide to walk out of the tent and let somebody else entertain. It wasn't my circus, and definitely not my monkeys.

No one was coming to rescue me.

I was the prince, princess, horse and carriage. I already had everything I needed to make a move. I just needed to take action if I was to achieve the greatest version of myself in this life.

At this point, I hate to break it to you, but unfortunately...

No one will come save you.

I know, terrible things may have happened to you. There's no denying that. Life has a way of roughing us up from time to time. Maybe you graduated during the worst job market in decades. Perhaps you were deserted at the altar. Or your less-deserving-but-better-bootlicking colleague got the promotion you were banking on. The list is long and the pain doesn't get any better. I get it. The fact is...

Life is unfair and the cards we are dealt with are not always fair either.

No one can choose the family they are born into or the environment they grow up in. But, thankfully, we can work to change what we don't like. You don't have to accept the cards you were dealt with and what you may have presumed to be your fate. No matter where you are in life, young or old, wrinkle-free or wrinkle-faced, it's never too late to go after what you want in life or to be who you want to be.

You might be thinking: *Yeah...whatever.* I've felt the same way too. But being dismissive won't miraculously change your situation.

What I know for sure is that...

It is too early to give in and give up.

You can keep on sulking, blaming others and complaining about your circumstances while the people you deem responsible for it are out there living their best lives, likely unbothered. Until you decide to act on something that's important to you, nothing will change.

Why be a passenger in your life when you are meant to be the pilot?

We play the waiting game for too long. Yes, there are instances where patience is required. But for many of us, we wait for seasons to be in our favor. You know, the big break, the perfect moment to start. We let others dictate our "why's" and "how's" while we sit silently on the sidelines in the passenger seat. We hope that tomorrow will be better. The reality is...

*Tomorrow will come and go. It might not be what you
want unless you create it.*

You don't have to have everything figured out but you need to stop going full speed down the same path, knowing very well where it's going to lead you—back to the same old crusty ranch.

Finding yourself in a soul-destroying job, a dead-end relationship or deep in debt is not the end of the world. You can decide to take another path. You can make other choices. It's only the end if you decide that's all you deserve. And deep down, you know you deserve only the best. The "best" is what brings you joy, contentment and what helps you grow and thrive. If that's not the case, well...

*You owe it to yourself to put up, show up and show off
your life.*

The opportunity to have a great life, and the decision to take steps toward achieving that life, reside in your hands.

American psychologist Albert Ellis summarized this best when he said, "The best years of your life are the ones in which you decide your problems are your own. You do not blame them on your mother, the economy or the president. You realize that you control your own destiny. Empowerment happens when you face the profound responsibility you have for your own life."

So, what is it going to be?

BRAVER STORY

With

DWAYNE "THE ROCK" JOHNSON

How did Dwayne "The Rock" Johnson go from jobless and broke to one of the biggest names in the entertainment industry?

Dwayne's phenomenal career has often been attributed to his work ethic, resilience and determination. While these are essential ingredients for any successful endeavor, it all started once he took responsibility for his life.

At the age of 22, he was dropped from the Canadian Football League just two days after making his professional debut. His dream of being a professional football player was crushed in an instant. A dream he had been working towards for ten long years!

Now left with just $7 in his pocket, he had no choice but to go back home and move in with his parents. In the weeks that followed Dwayne became gradually more depressed by his situation. But then something in him clicked.

In that moment, he *decided* that he was going to turn his life around. He realized what many of us need to learn too: that no one was coming to give him a great life. It was up to him and him alone to build that great life.

So, Dwayne started training again and became a professional wrestler, winning multiple titles. He then turned his hand to acting and quickly became an international movie star. Reflecting on his journey, Dwayne said, "You gotta have faith that the one thing you wanted to happen oftentimes is the best thing that never happened."

Keep going!

A BRAVER YOU

In Action

FIND YOUR ACCOUNTABILITY PARTNER

Taking life by the horns and remaining focused on your journey requires more than just holding yourself to account. As we all know, having the best of intentions is simply not enough—life has a way of derailing us along the way. That's why you need an **accountability partner**.

So, for your first *In Action* exercise you need to recruit a suitable accountability partner.

- **What is an accountability partner?** This is someone you admire and are comfortable with. Someone who will hold you responsible for the decisions you make and the goals you set.

- **What makes a great accountability partner?** Your partner needs to be reliable and be willing to walk this journey with you. The person you pick shouldn't be afraid to tell you the truth and call you out when you're slacking.

- **How do I get started with my accountability partner?** Pick one habit you want to change, or a goal you want to accomplish, and share this with your accountability partner. Then decide how your progress will be measured and evaluated.

CHAPTER 2

Know Yourself

—

"You are very powerful, provided you know

how powerful you are."

—YOGI BAHAMAN

Have you ever hid inside a closet, hoping to emerge later as someone else? Sounds crazy, right? Still, that's what many of us do.

We attempt to go through life running away from our true selves. We become experts at adopting inauthentic personas. You can divorce everyone but yourself. I've tried. It's not possible, even with the best lawyers!

I know myself. Well, at least I thought I did. I have a birth certificate and a passport. I love seafood pasta and espresso without sugar. I can't stand ice cream and I can only stomach sparkling water. Yes, these are parts of my personality, but do they define me as a person?

HOW WELL DO YOU KNOW YOURSELF?

Knowing yourself is looking beyond your favorite treats and preferred yoga pose. The ancient Greeks encouraged each other to "know thyself" by engaging in introspection for self-knowledge purposes. This means becoming a conscious friend to yourself in order to cultivate the most authentic version of yourself. When you know yourself, it's much easier to set achievable goals. You'll develop a clearer sense of direction, giving you more control over your life.

When you know yourself, you become more confident. You'll feel more assured in the decisions you make. And if things don't go according to plan, you can change course without doubting yourself.

Now for the big question: do you truly know yourself? To help you answer that, see how many of these statements you can identify with:

- You change your behavior based on who you're around.

- You don't know what you want out of life.

- You let others take control of your life.

- You rely on others to make decisions for you.

- You put other people's priorities first and neglect your own.

- You internalize other people's beliefs and perceptions.

If this sounds like you, you're not alone!

THE ROAD TO SELF-KNOWLEDGE

It's risky not knowing who you are. A lack of self-knowledge could lead you to make choices that don't honor your authentic self. It could also cause you to feel insecure about the decisions you've already taken. But because you never took the time to hang out with yourself, your GPS is taking you to places you don't belong, with people you shouldn't be traveling with.

When I was younger, I habitually changed my personality to accommodate the people and the world around me. Over time I started to take other people's views more seriously, blocking out my voice. I had convinced myself that other people had it right and I had it wrong. After all, what could I possibly know?

A part of me was looking at others to tell me how to think, choose and feel. How many times did I say "yes" when I wanted to say "no"? How many times did I go somewhere I didn't want to be? How many times did I stay in places that no longer served me? I hopped on and off this merry-go-round consciously and unconsciously until my friend Cynthia confronted me about it.

I knew she was out to mess up the rest of my day the moment she cornered me on her patio. In her husky Nigerian "mom voice" she went straight for it. "What is it with you that you become someone else around different people? I don't know who you are anymore," she said while chopping up a big onion.

I don't know if it was the onion or her calling me out that made my eyes watery, but I was unprepared for that moment. "What do you mean?" I asked, feigning ignorance. With a *don't take me for stupid* stare, Cynthia walked to the kitchen and left me with my thoughts. In one fell swoop she had ruined both my makeup and the rest of my afternoon!

Looking back, I'm grateful for that moment. I wanted to justify my behavior by just doing what I got to do, especially when it allowed me to fit in. No big deal, I thought. "Adapt or die" became my mantra. Well, that's all I was doing. I acted like a chameleon. A little adjustment here, a little tweak there wouldn't hurt anyone, right? Wrong. I was seeking external approval instead of developing self-acceptance.

You will keep denying yourself
if you don't know yourself.

You are who you are. Accept it or deny it at your own risk. Every time you bury yourself, your opinions and your reality to fit someone else's narrative, you are effectively denying yourself. The energy you're investing in trying to shape and mold yourself into somebody you aren't, to suit other people's fantasies of who you need to be, is a waste of precious time. You'll just be repeating the same old mistakes and be stuck in the same old situations, all because you lack self-knowledge. It's hard to imagine that in a world with over 7 billion people there could be something unique that you can contribute. Being different is good. Being different is power. In the words of Dr. Seuss, "Today you are you, that is truer than true. There is no one alive who is youer than you."

But why aren't you youer than you?

Because we don't want to take the time to ask ourselves some difficult questions. We don't take the time to understand our patterns, motivations, values, likes and dislikes to find out who we really are. Instead, we end up being like leaves blown by the wind in every direction. We end up living according to other people's wishes and desires—everyone else's but our own. We seek happiness but never find it because we don't even know what makes us happy. We base our perception of joy on someone else's version of what it looks and feels like. So why don't we make time to get to know ourselves better? Well, if we're honest about it, the whole thing sounds like work. And we tend to associate work with discomfort. Could there be a better way to look at this?

THE GIFT IN KNOWING YOURSELF

Knowing yourself is like unwrapping a gift that will keep on giving. It's the most valuable investment you could make in your lifetime. Have you ever heard someone talk to you about a book they've read, and how the chapters and stories unfolded? Did you feel like you wanted to read that same book yourself? Getting to know yourself works in much the same way. Your self-worth is determined by your relationship with yourself, not the one your friends or family tell you that you should have.

You are like a book filled with wonders and treasures. Only by flipping through the chapters do you get to discover all that you are.

By genuinely getting to know yourself, you have the opportunity to explore wonders you may not even know live within you. The invaluable treasures that you hold within may foster a greater sense of wonder, boost your self-esteem and help you evolve. Knowing yourself enables you to stand firm in—and with—your choices. You're able to develop better habits and kick the unnecessary ones to the curb.

We tend to underestimate the importance of knowing ourselves. As a result, many of us go through each day reacting to events and just "getting by" rather than making conscious choices based on who we are and what we want. Sometimes, you will be privileged enough to have a caring friend or family member to spark that self-awareness, as in my case. In other instances, experiences will keep happening in your life to draw your attention to your lack of authenticity. It will be tempting to ignore them or find excuses to justify them in these cases. But it might be best to adopt the famous breakup line of "it's not you, it's me," and start taking steps to get to know yourself.

GETTING TO KNOW YOURSELF

The action of getting to know yourself won't unfold like an algebra calculation. And there's certainly no "seven steps of knowing yourself" that you can quickly run through and be done.

It's not a destination.

No one is going to give you a certificate of completion for knowing yourself. There won't be a celebration for this kind of graduation. And that's okay. The happiness, sense of direction and confidence you'll get will far outweigh even the best of celebrations. You're not some kind of wax figurine—and even those get a fresh coat of paint from time to time. Knowing yourself doesn't mean you're not allowed to change your mind or take different directions. Your life will take various twists and turns but getting to know yourself will help you withstand those unforeseen events. When you know yourself, you're in a better position to recognize when you've made a decision that's not aligned with your values. Getting to know yourself is about uncovering your deepest fears, doubts and insecurities.

If you don't know who you are, how are you supposed to know where to go?

To sum it all up, knowing yourself requires looking inward for answers that people or things won't give you. Self-awareness is the foundation that leads to acceptance, clarity and ultimately to realized ambitions. Knowing yourself is essential as it then sets the base for your "no's," your "yes's" and your "ugh's." The opportunities you'll take and the ones you'll turn down will depend heavily on who you think you are.

Here are some tips you could take to get to know yourself better:

IN ACTION: KNOW YOURSELF	
Instead of:	**Consider this:**
Not having goals and putting other people's priorities first and neglecting your own.	**What are your aspirations?** What interests you? What do you like to do? Write it all down and prioritize them.
Changing your behavior to adapt to people.	**Start telling yourself this**: "It is okay to be different." People who love you will accept the real you and those who won't, well that's not your problem.
Settling for things and people that you know don't deserve your time and energy.	**Start by identifying only one area in your life** where you feel you might be settling. Write down what you would like to see instead in three points. Take one point at the time to work on.

BRAVER TIP

By

DEEPAK CHOPRA

How do you know yourself and stay true to yourself? By paying attention to what and how you're experiencing things around you. Deepak Chopra believes that **your true self is confident, stable, has clarity about things and is not consumed by the ego-self.**

You know you're connected to your true self when you:

- Feel more centered in yourself, there's a sense of safety and bliss day by day. You accept yourself as you are.

- You also experience fewer negative emotions and more positive emotions like love, kindness and empathy.

As Chopra explained, any time you feel the opposite, you are no longer connected to your true self: "The person willing to be the most uncomfortable is not only the bravest but also rises the fastest."

A BRAVER YOU

In Action

MEET YOURSELF

Bring on the flashlights because it's all about **you** today. Grab a notebook, a pencil and an eraser. The goal is to jot down your interests, beliefs, values, habits and aspirations—anything that moves you.

- **Your interests:** are things you enjoy doing and like to give attention to.

- **Your values:** standards, ideals, principles that you live by.

- **Your habits:** things that you regularly do.

- **Your aspirations:** goals and objectives that you want to accomplish.

Draw four columns with these different headings and fill them up as much as you like. Write and erase as needed, don't overthink it. Then use all the words you wrote down to form full sentences and write a profile about yourself.

Don't know where to start?

Because I practice what I preach, I've done this exercise myself and provided a copy of my profile in the resources section at the back of the book. Once you're finished writing your profile, put it somewhere visible and easily accessible. I keep mine in my notebook on my nightstand and look at it from time to time. It serves as a reminder of what matters most to me—what I should do to honor my soul.

Remember, there's no right or wrong aspect of what you're writing. It's not about getting your notes validated. It's about discovering what makes you tick by reading about it and facing it on paper. Now over to you!

CHAPTER 3

Love Yourself

—

*"The fact that someone else loves you doesn't
rescue you from the project of loving yourself."*

—SAHAJ KOHLI

Love yourself they say. You see it everywhere. From posters and pop culture to social media. A constant reminder that the most important relationship we ought to have is the one with ourselves. But at the same time, we're also sold this notion that someone, from somewhere, will one day come and give you the love you've never experienced before. A love that will complete you. But the only person that can make you whole is YOU.

Love and war

My friend Logan and I wrote affirmations like "I love myself" and "I am enough" in bold colors all over our bathroom mirrors while living together. We could skip eating breakfast but under no circumstances were we to forgo our daily ritual of chanting these affirmations. We needed firm reminders that we were self-secure and that we loved ourselves. The irony was that to outsiders it was clear that self-love had left the building.

Of course we got a confidence boost from these affirmations. But it never lasted. The truth is no amount of positive affirmations could fix our lack of self-love. We should have known that for positive affirmations to have an impact, we first needed to believe in them. Deep down, we knew we did not love ourselves, and affirming it by faking it wasn't going to change it.

GOT SELF LOVE?

Loving yourself means that you have compassion, consideration and appreciation for your happiness and well-being. You love yourself unconditionally, secure in the knowledge that no matter what happens and no matter how you feel in the present moment, you are worthy. When you love yourself, you tend to take steps and actions to honor your body, mind and goals. When you don't have self-love, you will compromise on all the things you hold dear.

Do any of these statements ring true?

- You're constantly putting yourself down through your words, thoughts and actions.

- You struggle to remember the last time you put yourself first.

- You keep falling for toxic people.

- You give up on your goals too easily.

- You often think others are better than you.

- You neglect your physical and mental well-being.

- You don't invest in your growth.

Loving yourself is not a quick-fix solution. In Logan and I's case, we wanted a quick fix—a microwaveable type of fix. A mac and cheese type of fix. Fast, easy and painless. But what we were doing was like putting a bandage over an open wound. Even when an injury lays dormant, sooner or later, it opens up again and you certainly don't want it to spread and fester. And boy, did my wounds spread. It spread in the form of my love for other people's problems. I became a crusader for everyone's causes but my own. It seems as if I loved everyone else but myself. I took altruism and selflessness to reckless dimensions. I racked up the achievements, filled my time with responsibilities and busy-bodied myself with others' needs over my own. In the end, I overextended myself and started to look like Davy Jones from the Pirates of the Caribbean film series.

There is a "you" in "I love you."
Honor that.

There was barely a "no" in my vocabulary. Honoring my needs and dreams was selfish, and I was afraid of that selfish label. So, I went out of my way not to be labeled selfish. I wanted the brownie points that came with being labeled kind, gentle and caring. I earned a Ph.D. in "You before me" and was well on my way to my lifelong miseducation, until one day life decided to cancel that degree program.

It was an ordinary but soon-to-be-dramatic winter morning. I was sitting at my desk and replying to emails when I felt the first of many sharp pains in my chest. I remembered turning to my colleague, gesturing to her and muttering something along the lines of "something is wrong" and that I needed to go to the hospital. After a battery of tests were performed, a doctor nonchalantly announced that they all came back negative. He explained what I experienced was simply a panic attack. *A what?* Did he say the words "panic attack"? These two words are not my friends. But the seriousness of the doctor's face soon made me realize this was no joke. He asked questions about my lifestyle, made some recommendations and prescribed some medicine. I was discharged back into my life.

It was indeed a wake-up call. I have since learned to practice Jim Rohn's idea of, "If you will take care of me, I will take care of you." But now I say, "I will take care of me for you, if you will take care of you for me." And you can do that too.

WHY SELF-LOVE IS KEY?

We often use the expression "this too shall pass" to comfort and uplift others when the going gets tough. A panic attack shall pass, sadness shall pass, being tired will pass too. But if there's one thing that you should not let pass you by, it's self-love. It's something you should put a ring on and make sure that you never divorce. It must stay with you, and the two of you shall be one till the end of time. Self-love is about making a life-long commitment to yourself first.

You may think that self-love is egotistical and selfish. I used to be one of those people but learned that self-love is not just necessary, it's critical. Self-love is not about thinking you are better than someone else in a narcissistic way. Self-love is taking care of your own needs first and prioritizing your well-being before anyone else's. Learning to love yourself also requires raw honesty instead of taping affirmations all over the house like Logan and I did. You need to embrace uncovering all the brokenness and flaws to accept yourself fully as you are now, not as you wish to be one day.

GET ON THE SELF-LOVE TRAIN

You don't just wake up one day and love yourself. True self-love takes practice and demands consistency. It requires commitment and understanding that you won't get where you want to be in life without loving yourself first.

Here are some practical steps that may help you cultivate more self-love:

IN ACTION: LOVING YOURSELF	
Instead of:	**Consider this:**
Putting yourself last and others first.	**Learn and embrace being compassionate to yourself.** It's important to show and express concern for yourself just as you will do for others.
Not appreciating your own abilities and questioning your self-worth.	**Make a list.** Write down your accomplishments, things you love about yourself and things you think you are pretty good at. Read this list often.
Doing everything for everybody and forgetting yourself.	**Invest in yourself** by doing more of things you love and less of the things you hate.

BRAVER TIP

By

LOUISE HAY

Louise Hay's mirror work concept is based on the premise that the most powerful affirmations we can say are the ones done in front of the mirror. Why? Because the mirror will reflect back the feelings that we have about ourselves. In essence, you can't fake it with your mirror. The mirror will show you the truth.

How do you do it? Your mirror becomes your companion in facing yourself. For example:

- When something good has happened, stand in front of your mirror and say, "Wow, well done. You did it. Look at that, you rock!"

- If something terrible happens to you, you still go to the mirror and say, "I still love you. Nothing has changed. This situation is temporary and it will pass. I love you."

A BRAVER YOU

In Action

SELF-COMPASSION: THE KINDNESS LETTER

When you have compassion for others you express empathy, care and non-judgment when they are suffering, facing setbacks and going through change. Self-compassion is no different. The same kindness and care we freely give to others should be part of our personal toolkit. Self-compassion is about being kind to yourself, finding and nurturing the friend within just as you encourage the friend outside. How can you boost the compassion you have for yourself? There is no cure-all but you can practice more self-compassion by merely being kinder to yourself. So, today we are going to practice being kind to ourselves.

How? I want you to write a letter to yourself:

- **Write it from the perspective of one of your dear friends** or family members. In this letter, you'll discuss your weaknesses, strengths and what you perceive as imperfections.

- As you write the letter, **infuse it** with kindness, love and understanding.

After writing the letter, what do you do with it? You can carry it with you in your journal and read it every day. Check out my version of this exercise in the resources section at the end of the book.

CHAPTER 4

Believe In Yourself

—

"The fact that someone else loves you doesn't rescue you from the project of loving yourself."

—SAHAJ KOHLI

Do you know someone that studied one thing but seems to have supernatural talents for another? I do.

Let me tell you about my friend Kekeli who is a formidable lawyer. She is an even more impressive negotiator and, as I found out on a recent vacation with her, she could moonlight exceptionally well as a motivational speaker and preacher. It was meant to be a relaxing girls-only vacation. A time to shop, reflect and explore Tokyo and the rich heritage of Japanese culture. Pure relaxation. I needed time off from my demanding job as a business strategist, and when the opportunity came, I jumped on it. I was to regret it pretty soon though.

We were taking a stroll down a busy street in Shibuya when Kekeli stopped me dead in my tracks to deliver the first part of her sermon, "You will never be ready. You just have to start," she said while adjusting the straps on her bag. "I believe in you. We all believe in you. You have to take the leap and start. Stop waiting for a sign and just take action." She stopped walking, turned around, looked at me and said, "There are people less talented than you who are making it happen. Now is your time, girl! For everything, there is a season. A time for every activity under heaven and..." I cut her off. "Yes, a time to plant and a time to harvest. Yes, pastor. Halleluiah!" I replied sarcastically while clapping my hands and rolling my eyes.

You see, Kekeli loved Ecclesiastes 3:1-8 with a capital L. But all I wanted to do that morning was go through the buzzing streets of Shibuya and get through my shopping list of must-have beauty products. Was it too much to ask to keep the conversation light? But here she was, giving me a lecture about believing in myself. But did I actually believe in myself?

DO YOU BELIEVE IN YOURSELF?

If I were to be brutally honest with myself, I had deep-rooted self-limiting beliefs and Kekeli knew it. Self-limiting beliefs are simply self-critical and unhealthy thoughts that hold you back from reaching your true potential. Over time these beliefs conspire to erode your confidence and prevent you from experiencing real happiness.

The list of self-limiting beliefs we carry around is long. Do any of these descriptions apply to you?

- You are always finding reasons why you can't do things.

- You tell yourself that you don't have enough experience or qualifications.

- You think everything needs to be perfect before you start, or you start something and never finish it.

- You think that you are too old, small, big or poor to get started on your goals.

- You don't think that you can be happy and successful.

If any of these beliefs resonate with you, you are not alone. I've been there. In my case, my self-limiting beliefs showed up in the form of having many creative ideas but seldom taking action to realize them. And when I did, I would stop halfway and never pursue them to the end.

WHERE DO SELF-LIMITING BELIEFS COME FROM?

For many people, self-limiting beliefs manifest from their childhood. But you may have formed these negative beliefs at any time. There is a psychological principle called belief perseverance that explains how we tend to hold our beliefs as valid even if there is significant evidence proving that the view is wrong. So, we go through life holding onto beliefs that don't serve us, and most of the time, end up hindering us.

After college, I attempted to launch a business but it failed. I lost all the money I invested into it and my self-esteem took a massive knock. I convinced myself that I was just not cut out for entrepreneurship. Even when I saw people around me launching successful side-hustles, I was sure that I couldn't do it myself. My favorite line was, "Some people are business people and then there is me ... a nobody." Kekeli could clearly see through my BS, and her bringing it up freaked me out.

Many of us are unable to move from the life we have to the life we want. We are stuck and lack faith in our abilities. We have surrendered to self-limiting beliefs, drowning in fears and self-sabotaging behaviors while nurturing catastrophic predictions. We allow thoughts to control us instead of controlling our thoughts, and then we wonder why our lives seem to be in the gutter.

YOUR MIND = YOUR SUPERPOWER

Your mind is so powerful that it will control you if you don't master it. Your thoughts affect your perception—and eventually the interpretation—of your reality. Yet few of us take control of our thoughts. What we think and entertain as thoughts influences how we feel, behave and react to circumstances we are confronted with.

It usually starts small. You apply for one job and get rejected. You apply for five, then ten and all you get are big fat "no's". Soon, you'll start thinking there's something seriously wrong with you and begin to dread applying for any more. You start thinking, "What's the use? I will be rejected again," and soon enough your beliefs turn into self-fulling prophecies. More rejection comes your way, leaving you shattered. You end up parking your dream of working for a big company, moving to a new city and living your desired life. Now you start blaming everybody. Your parents. Your boss. The economy. Your date of birth. Anything and everything. However, the truth is ...

> *"There is nothing outside of yourself that can ever enable you to get better, stronger, richer, quicker or smarter. Everything is within. Everything exists. Seek nothing outside of yourself."*
>
> —MIYAMOTO MUSASHI

Your mind is either your ally or your enemy. Every day we get the opportunity to choose which camp we are playing in. We can also decide to take hold of our thoughts and not let them play ping-pong with us. "The mind is a flexible mirror, you'll have to adjust it to see a better world," proclaims spiritual teacher Amit Ray. By adjusting your mindset you'll not only be able to commit to your goals and take action, you'll ultimately be able to change your life. It might take a bit of work and time to eradicate deep-rooted thought patterns, but why keep entertaining thoughts that don't serve you? After all, it's possible to train your brain to think differently.

It's time to get our thoughts on a leash. Shall we?

HOW TO LEVEL UP YOUR MINDSET

Even though it might take some time for you to start smashing your goals, by changing your thoughts you'll soon be able to get out of your rut and forge new pathways. While there are many techniques on how you can level up your mindset, here are some that you could adopt:

IN ACTION: BELIEVING IN YOURSELF	
Instead of:	**Consider this:**
Using negative words about yourself.	**Focus on changing your self-talk.** Using positive words will empower you for success.
Thinking that everything has to be perfect before you start.	**Embrace getting things done** instead of wanting things to be perfect.
Focusing on all the things that are going wrong or could go wrong.	**Remind yourself** of your inner abilities and the skills you have. Make a list if needed.

BRAVER TIP

By

SHAD HELMSTETTER

Shad Helmstetter, a pioneer in self-talk, believes that we should all engage in daily self-talk. Our self-talk has the power to change the things that we would like to change, even if we haven't been able to do so in the past. Self-talk is about re-wiring the old program and learning the language of responsibility. To change your self-talk from negative to positive, Helmstetter suggests doing the following:

STEP 1:

Identify what you are saying about yourself right now. Start by monitoring what you say about yourself daily. Write it down to keep track.

STEP 2:

Notice when you are saying negative things about yourself and reframe those thoughts by saying the opposite. Essentially turning the negative into a positive. It might be weird at first, but just like your brain got used to being negative, it will become positive.

STEP 3:

Every morning listen to a positive self-talk recording of 10-15 minutes on a topic you find motivating. Stay consistent for at least 2-3 weeks.

I've shared more information in the resources section at the end of the book to help you get going with step 3.

NEGATIVE SELF-TALK STOPPING TECHNIQUE

Shifting negative thoughts to positive ones is easier said than done. But you can learn how to silence your negative self-talk by using the technique below.

S-TOP

Mentally tell yourself "stop!" to give you the opportunity to address the thought and interrupt the cycle.

O-BSERVE

Observe what you are saying to yourself and how it is making you feel.

S-HIFT

Shift your cognitive, emotional, behavioral response by using positive coping skills and techniques.

A BRAVER YOU

In Action

WALKING THE TALK (CONTINUED)

The S-0-S negative self-talk stopping technique is worth remembering and adopting.

What I want you to focus on today is the **"Observing"** and **"Shifting"** parts.

- **Your day task**: you observe and record everything you said about yourself during the day. Don't just make a mental note of it—you will eventually forget. Make sure you write it down so you can remember all of them.

- **Your evening task**: find some quiet time to sit down and rephrase all the negative things you noted down into positive talk.

Repeat the positive talk 2-3 times after finishing the exercise. The more you practice this exercise, the more you will see your self-talk change.

CHAPTER 5

Live Your Truth

—

"I never wanted to be on any billionaires list. I
never define myself by net worth. I always try
to define myself by my values."

—HOWARD SCHULTZ

Siri, what are my five most important values? Answer: "Here is what I found," and she gives me a list of random websites about values.

What did I expect from the voice assistant on my phone? Not much, honestly. Laugh all you want but that's what most of us do: we pick random values and adopt them as our own. My failed experiment with Siri may be extreme and laughable, but let me ask you: what are your values? Let's make it specific: what are your top five values? If you're scratching your head, making confused faces or can only come up with one or two, that's okay. Hopefully, by the time you finish reading this, you'll better understand what values are and why you need to live by yours.

Ah, good ol' values! We all grew up hearing about them. Our parents encouraged us to uphold them, and even companies have values that they shout about from the rooftops of their headquarters to appeal to their employees and customers. But how many of us know what it means? Better yet, how many of us live up to them?

WHAT ARE VALUES?

A standard definition of values is: "principles that help you decide what is right and wrong and how to act in various situations". I like to think about values as guideposts, principles that help me live my truth and influence my decisions and actions. They help determine how I allocate my focus and form my opinions. Your values define you and you alone. Elvis Presley once said, "Values are like fingerprints. Nobody's are the same, but you leave 'em all over everything you do." Someone may value adventure and I love security. That doesn't mean that my values are better. It just means that you are unlikely to convince me to go skydiving with you. My character is a bit on the predictable, square-box side and that's okay.

WHY YOU SHOULD KNOW YOUR VALUES

You are what you think, but even more so, what you value. Values define who you are, not who you think you should be. Your set of values is like a mirror you hold to your face. It will reflect back and certainly show you when you are out of sync with yourself.

"Values aren't buses ... They're not supposed to get you anywhere. They're supposed to define who you are."
—JENNIFER CRUSIE

The values you hold so dearly and act on also define your character. When we say that a particular person is kind, we're saying that they are considerate and generous towards others. And your character, the essence of who you are, those distinctive qualities that you have, can either take you far in life or hold you back. Have you ever heard people talking about someone with a "bad character"? Definitely not a label worth having.

KNOWING YOUR VALUES ALSO GIVES YOU CLARITY.

And clarity, my friend, will help you attract what you want in this life. Do you want more clarity in your career, your relationships, your goals? Clarify your values first. You'll then be able to make decisions that are right for you in all aspects of your life.

"It is not hard to make decisions when you know what your values are."
—ROY DISNEY

Your values guide you to who you truly are. They light the way to the path of personal and professional success. So how come so many of us don't know what our values are? We've heard about values all our lives but still don't know them. In other cases, some people *think* they know their values. Most of us are usually not aware of our values. But whether you know your values or not, you are currently living by some values. The question is: are those the values you want?

KNOWING AND LIVING YOUR VALUES

Knowing your values is important but do you know what matters even more? Living up to your values. Having the courage to live your values is not easy but it's the only way through. Because we share different values from others, we are sometimes afraid to voice our concerns about a particular situation because we risk being judged or condemned. So, we go with the status quo. We end up compromising our values and changing our non-negotiables. And we think that if we bend once, we are just doing it that one time.

But what you tolerate, you accept, and what you accept is
what you become.

And living with a version of yourself that you don't like will give you stress and cause unhappiness. How do I know? I've been there. You can lie to people and fake it all the way if you want but whenever you're not living up to your values or compromising them, you will feel discomfort and be out of touch with yourself. Want to live a life with no regrets? Want to become the person you are meant to be? Get clear on what values are meaningful to you, commit to them and act on them. Where do you go to find your values? There is no museum of values and no guidebook you can buy to find it. It requires exploring:

IN ACTION: FINDING YOUR VALUES

Instead of:	Consider this:
Adopting and living by other people's values. Picking random values.	**Take 10 minutes** to reflect and find your values. **Reflect back on your highest and lowest moments.** These experiences might reveal your key values.

BRAVER TIP

By

JAMES CLEAR

James Clear is the best-selling author of Atomic Habits, a must-read on how to develop new and sustainable habits. Among many other tips that Clear has shared over the years, the one that stuck the most with me has been the Integrity Report. As he describes it, the Integrity Report is an exercise that helps him keep his values top of mind each year. The Integrity Report helps him answer this question: **"Am I living like the type of person I claim to be?"**

There are three sections in the Integrity Report, based on these questions:

- What are the core values that drive your life and work? (Clarification on values)

- How are you living and working with integrity right now? (Measures of success)

- How can you set a higher standard in the future? (accountability)

I like how straightforward this is, and it's an approach I've adopted to help keep myself in check. I know we've jumped the gun a little here—you won't be able to be accountable unless you define your values first. So, let's get into that!

A BRAVER YOU

In Action

RENDEZVOUS WITH VALUES

Get your notebook out because you have a crucial *rendezvous:* you're on a quest to discover your core values. If you already know your values, fast-forward to step five. Ready?

STEP 1:

Go to the back of the book for a list of values that can guide your brainstorming. Although not exhaustive, it will get you started. Select and write down the words that feel like a value to you.

STEP 2:

Put your chosen values into groups. Try to limit your groupings to five each.

STEP 3:

Label each group. Pick a word within each group that can be a representative and the title for the group.

STEP 4:

Add a verb before the word to turn it into an actionable value.

STEP 5:

Live your values. What's the best way to make sure you use your values as a compass in your day-to-day life? Write them down in your daily journal and on post-it notes that you can stick at your desk so you can see them every day.

CHAPTER 6

The Approval Fix

—

"Seeking validation is the same as saying, tell me who I am! Tell me what I'm worth! Tell yourself."

—ANONYMOUS

Growing up, I was fascinated by some of the older girls in my neighborhood. They wore whatever they wanted, did their hair however they wished, and had a *je ne sais quoi* attitude that made me envious. They seemed to come and go as they pleased, and I envied their freedom as a teenager.

No one seemed to be the boss of them, and they could be whoever they wanted, or at least so it seemed. My hidden admiration for these girls was discounted with the horror on my mom's face anytime we encountered them in the neighborhood. In these instances, my mother would lift her arms to the sky and angrily say, "God forbid you become like those girls. These 'do-nothing' girls...hmm, they are just waiting for someone to marry them." With one hand on her hip, and the other hand pointing her finger at me, she would look at me directly in the eyes and say, "Don't ever be a 'do nothing' girl. You are a smart girl, and you come from a good family. Always remember that."

I wanted to interject and asked what a "do nothing girl" meant but I knew better than to argue with my mother. Anyone with African parents understands that the fastest way to clap-back season is to talk back to your parents! As children, the first two words you master quickly are "yes" and "amen".

So I grew up wanting to be far from a "do nothing girl". I wanted to be a smart girl, *that* perfect girl. I came up with my recipe for being that girl: 3 cups of perfection, 2 cups of approval-seeking and a dash of people-pleasing to ensure that the room smelled of eager perfectionism at all times. It took me years to realize that I was an approval seeker and a people pleaser. No one pointed it out to me, mind you. The sadness and emptiness I felt when I made decisions that did not honor my authentic self were enough for me to recognize that something needed to change.

YOU ARE GIVING AWAY YOUR POWER

Do any of these statements speak to you? (check any that apply)

- You change your point of view often to suit others.

- You always say "yes" and agree to do things even when you just want to say "no".

- You find yourself asking for permission unnecessarily.

- You do things just to fit in and avoid confrontations even though they are not aligned with your values.

- You have trouble setting boundaries or you are afraid to put up boundaries for fear of losing people.

- You feel guilty when you stand up for yourself.

If you see yourself in any of the above examples, you are an approval seeker.

WHY DO WE SEEK APPROVAL?

It's human nature to seek approval. But why do we do this? Maslow's hierarchy of needs theory teaches us that feeling loved, belonging to something and having self-esteem are central to who we are.

We are wired to desire relationships and connections. Feeling supported, loved and appreciated helps us navigate the ups and downs of life. And we want our family and our peers to recognize our achievements—this satisfies our need to belong to social groups, whether offline or online.

In essence, there's nothing wrong with our desire for emotional and physical security and to be part of a tribe. This is, after all, what makes us human. And while there's nothing wrong with asking for advice to inform our decisions, there's a fine line between that and always seeking validation from other people. If you continuously need approval from others, you are giving them power over you. And no one else but you is deserving of that much power.

Our quest for approval also comes from our conditioning as children. As children, we sought permission from our parents on what to do, how to behave and things to say. We are rewarded and praised if we do as we are told, and we are chastised if we don't. So, we quickly learn what to do to be loved and what to avoid. As a child, you knew that a nod and a smile were signs that you were doing well. A frown, however, was an indication that you were going down the wrong path and that you should quickly change course. And sometimes doing what was expected of you came with candies, new toys or playtime. This is how we become conditioned to seek out validation from friends, family and even strangers. And when we don't get it, we try to do everything to make people see it. This leads us to do things we might ordinarily not do, even if it means changing parts of our selves just to get it.

Always seeking validation from others is like handing someone a blank checkbook and letting them make withdrawals from your account whenever they like.

When you're always seeking validation, you're creating the impression that you don't value yourself. You are giving all your power away. You are putting other people's opinions, approval and acceptance of you above what you think of yourself and your life. Relying on others to support your value is unhealthy and unsustainable—it creates anxiety in addition to emotional and physical fatigue.

Defining your worthiness through other's approval is sabotage.

How so? You may have dreams but instead of working on them, you procrastinate. You are so fearful of making mistakes and being judged that you don't do anything. The result? You miss opportunities, you develop more negative thoughts and your need for validation intensifies. The greatest act of service you can render to yourself is simply to honor your needs, your wants and your most authentic self. As the writer Richelle E. Goodrich said, "What do you mean I have to wait for someone's approval? I'm someone. I approve." Approve of yourself unapologetically. Do you!

BREAK UP WITH APPROVAL SEEKING BEHAVIORS

Someone once said that if outside validation is your only source of nourishment, you will feel hunger for the rest of your life. Nobody wants this type of hunger, so committing to changing our approval-seeking behaviors is the only way to go. But as with any ingrained habits, commitment, time and effort are required to get us there.

While there is no one-size-fits-all strategy for change, here is a good starting point to taking your power back.

IN ACTION: AVOID APPROVAL-SEEKING BEHAVIOR

Instead of:	Consider this:
Saying "yes" when you really want to say "no".	**Establish healthy** and deliberate boundaries with people.
Feeling like a victim and blaming others.	**Keep a journal and/or speak** to a therapist to uncover the roots of the approval-seeking behavior.
Letting others make decisions for your life.	**Learn to trust yourself** and take responsibility for your choices.
Focusing on everyone else's needs. Getting upset and feeling rejected when people disagree with you.	**Embrace self-care.** Set goals for yourself and focus on them. Learn how to agree to disagree. Always remember that it's not personal.

BRAVER TIP

By

WAYNE DYER

"What you think of me is none of my business" is among Wayne Dyer's most famous quotes, and one we should perhaps all adopt. The internationally-recognized motivational speaker and author believes that the first thing we must all come to terms with is that we will never be able to please everyone. There will always be people who will be unhappy by what we do and how we choose to live our lives.

Here are five top strategies from Dyer to eliminate approval-seeking behavior:

- **Face disapproval**: when you face disapproval, tell yourself that it has nothing to do with you. What others think, say or do has nothing do with your self-worth.

- **Others' perceptions**: remind yourself that peoples' perceptions have no power over you unless you allow them to.

- **Avoid manipulation**: when you feel as though someone is trying to manipulate you by withholding approval, don't be afraid to speak up. And don't change your stance just so that you can get their approval.

- **Train yourself**: seek out people who will disapprove of things you say or do and train yourself to take a stand for what you believe in.

- **Don't argue:** avoid trying to convince others at all costs. Believe in yourself and your viewpoints.

A BRAVER YOU

In Action

ESTABLISH BOUNDARIES

We'll get into doing our work on boundaries in a moment, but I first want to discuss what boundaries are and why they are so important.

Boundaries are a way of communicating to others how we want to be treated. Boundaries are about making choices in your best interests, they determine who you allow in your space and what sort of behavior you will tolerate. Setting boundaries is the ultimate form of self-respect and self-love. And you don't owe anyone an explanation for your boundaries—they are yours for a reason. If anyone gets upset because of them, that's their problem and they don't deserve to be in your life.

Boundaries are personal and reflect your values. They can be physical (privacy, sexual orientation, your body), emotional and intellectual (behaviors, choices, sense of responsibility). Establishing healthy boundaries—and getting rid of unhealthy ones—has several benefits:

- You'll become more assertive.

- You'll become more comfortable when asking for your needs to be met.

- You'll experience less anger and resentment by no longer having people walk all over you.

- You'll take better care of yourself and become more self-aware.

Now that we've cleared up what boundaries are and why you need them, let's dive into our work for the day.

Establishing effective boundaries will depend on your set of values. So, this is a values-based exercise. If you haven't gone through the values exercise in Chapter 5 yet, I recommend that you first work through that and then return to this exercise.

MY BOUNDARIES

Knowing and setting your boundaries is essential to living a stress-free and happy life. In order to establish your boundaries, you need to know your values. How-to: Based on your values, you write down who you are(for example: If one of your value is creativity, you'll write" I am creative." Then, still based on your values, write down what you will accept and not accept.

My values are:

_____
_____
_____
_____
_____
_____
_____
_____
_____
_____
_____
_____

I am:

_____
_____
_____
_____
_____
_____
_____
_____
_____
_____
_____
_____

I will allow

_____
_____
_____
_____
_____
_____
_____
_____
_____
_____
_____
_____

I will not allow:

_____
_____
_____
_____
_____
_____
_____
_____
_____
_____
_____
_____

CHAPTER 7

The Emotion Code

—

"Self-control is strength. Calmness is mastery. You have to get to a point where your mood doesn't shift based on the insignificant actions of someone else. Don't allow others to control the direction of your life. Don't allow emotions to overpower your intelligence."

—MORGAN FREEMAN

I am not afraid to feel what I need to feel. Some may say that I feel excessively. Well, I made peace with the fact that I'm sensitive and tend to feel things deeply. I have a loud laugh and a piercing cry. Even when I try to hide my ugly cries, I wouldn't be surprised if they are heard from Cape Town to Cairo. But there is a difference between feeling your emotions and letting your emotions feel you, no pun intended. You can welcome your feelings but the fastest way to a crash is to let your emotions take over your life. You feel me?

WHO IS IN CHARGE?

During our lives we are bound to encounter various emotional challenges. Positive and negative emotions are all part of our human experience. At times, our emotions can be overwhelming. Instead of owning our negative emotions and managing them, sometimes we allow them to run rampant and boss us around. These negative emotions become uncontrollable waves that can throw us overboard. They shake us right and left, up and down and in whichever direction they send us, we go. Letting our emotions take control like that can lead to problems in our personal and professional relationships in both the short and long run.

Do any of these sound familiar? (check any that apply)

- You regret what you say after saying it.
- You tend to react first and think later.
- You swear by instant gratification and have no self-control.
- You ruminate over situations before or after they happen.
- You act negatively and hurt people (emotionally and physically) when you're upset.

WE NEED EMOTIONS

The word emotion comes from a French word that translates to "move out, remove, agitate". It's fitting then that our emotions are powerful enough to move us forward, backward or can cause us to get stuck. We are human beings and we have emotions for a reason. Emotions play an essential part in how we relate to and experience the world around us. Good or bad, emotions allow us to thrive, survive and expand. Emotions drive our actions, help us make decisions and help us connect with other people. They are necessary and are part of who we are. There will never be a point in life where you don't have them. You need your emotions. There are three parts to an emotion. The first is the physical feeling, how you feel in your body. The second part is how you interpret the event. That's why you and I can go through the same situation but our reactions can be different. The third part is the behavior that comes with the emotion. For example, going ballistic when you get stuck in a traffic jam.

TO FEEL OR NOT TO FEEL

Sometimes we try to numb our emotions with external things that we think can soothe us. We overindulge in food, binge-watch TV, gamble away the money we don't have or turn into pharmacists—all of this in the hope of not having to face our issues. By refusing to confront our problems, we allow these emotions to linger and we end up becoming slaves to them. Emotions serve as regulators to light your path and warn you when you are going the wrong way. Yet we treat emotions like gremlins—strange creatures that we let out of the bag but then need to reel in and hide.

I don't know how having emotions became a crime. It seems like we live in a world where we need to be stronger, better and faster with everything, including processing (or not) our emotions. You're supposed to feel but not so much that you'll appear weak. You are supposed to feel but don't embarrass yourself in the process. You are supposed to feel but do it quickly please. The truth is you can't get rid of your emotions and don't even think of suppressing them—it's harmful to the body and soul. When you're feeling something, people will tell you to "just get over it", to "get a grip" or to "calm down". These suggestions often come from a well-meaning and loving place— they are a way of telling you that you are throwing an adult tantrum and that you should control yourself.

While "getting over it" and "getting a grip" may seem like the best actions to take, they are very...

DANGEROUS AND UNHEALTHY

A study by the University of Texas found that bottling up one's emotions can make you more aggressive. It can also create psychological distress, depression and anxiety. If you don't allow yourself to feel or talk about what you're experiencing, these emotions can show up in other aspects of your life. For example, let's say you're upset with one of your friends and don't resolve the matter. Fast forward a couple of weeks and you lash out at one of your colleagues for no apparent reason. You don't understand what just happened. Your colleague is hurt and you are labeled a "crazy person", making the interactions with your team weird.

Ouch. You've got to take the time to accept and heal whatever emotion you feel or else you could die (worst case scenario) from carrying unprocessed emotions around. A study by the Harvard School of Public Health and the University of Rochester showed that emotional suppression increases one's chance of premature death from all causes by up to 35%. It seems like we can't win. We are crucified for showing emotion but if we bottle it up we face the possibility of death! So, what can we do about it?

SEEK EMOTIONAL BALANCE

Managing your emotions isn't the same as suppressing them. Ignoring your sadness or pretending you don't feel pain won't make those emotions go away. Unaddressed emotional wounds are likely to get worse over time. And there's a good chance suppressing your feelings will cause you to turn to unhealthy coping skills like overindulging in food or alcohol. Balancing your emotions means that you allow yourself to feel whatever you feel in the moment. This requires you to acknowledge your emotions and label how you feel. You may not be able to control the events and people around you, but if you're able to manage your emotions, you'll better be able to control your feelings.

If you want to feel happier and more in control of your life, pay attention to how you handle your emotions. It may be easier said than done, but here are a few suggestions to help you get started in managing your emotions effectively:

IN ACTION: MANAGING YOUR EMOTIONS

Instead of:	Consider this:
Reacting first and thinking later.	**Practice the 10-second rule**. Pause and take a deep breath. Walk away from the situation for a short period of time. Practice deep breathing and mindfulness techniques to help you transcend heavy emotional moments.
Indulging in instant gratification	**Remember the big picture**. Define your short-term and long-term goals. Keep a visual display of your goals close by so you'll be less tempted to act impulsively
Ruminating over things and actions you took.	**Write down what is bothering you** and see what you have control over. Try to take action to achieve a better outcome in the future.
Not listening to your emotions.	**Learn how to recognize** what your emotions are telling you (see below).

LISTEN TO YOUR EMOTIONS

BITTERNESS	shows you where you need to heal, where you're still holding judgments on others and yourself.
RESENTMENT	shows you where you you're living in the past and not allowing the present to be as it is.
DISCOMFORT	shows you what you need to pay attention right now to what's happening, because you're being given the opportunity to change, to do something different than you typically do it.
ANGER	shows you what you're passionate about, where your boundaries are, and what you believe needs to change about the world.
DISAPPOINTMENT	shows you that you tried for something, that you did not give in to apathy, that you still care.
GUILT	shows you that you're still living life in other people's expectations of what you should do.
SHAME	shows you that you're internalizing other people's beliefs about who should be (or who you are) and that you need to reconnect with yourself.
ANXIETY	shows you that you need to wake up, right now, and that you need to be present, that you're stuck in the past and living in fear of the future.
SADNESS	shows you the depth of your feeling, the depth of your care for others and this world.

BRAVER TIP

By

THE GOTTMAN INSTITUTE

Learning how to manage difficult emotions like anger, fear, confusion and sadness is key to living a happy, healthy and prosperous life.

Here are six strategies from the Gottman Institute on how to deal with difficult emotions:

1. **Become aware of the emotion:** identify where you feel the tension in your body. Don't push the emotion away or try to bottle it up.

2. **Identify and label:** you can only face what you know. State out loud, if necessary, what you're feeling. For example, "This is sadness" or "I feel sad".

3. **Accept the emotion:** don't deny it but rather give compassion to yourself for feeling the emotion. Remember you are feeling the emotion, you are not the emotion.

4. **Remember that it's temporary:** feelings come and go so be kind to yourself. Welcome those feelings when they do come, they will eventually go away again.

5. **Introspect:** once the feeling has gone away, take time to ask yourself these questions: "What triggered me?" and "Why do I feel this way?" These two questions will help you figure out the root cause behind your emotions.

6. **Let go of control:** emotions send messages and it's our role to listen. Don't try to control your emotions but do listen.

COUNTDOWN TO CALMNESS

The countdown to calmness or the 5-4-3-2-1 exercise is a simple yet effective way to use all your five senses to stop unpleasant emotions in their tracks and bring you back into the present moment. Even if you are not feeling any difficult emotion right now, don't skip this exercise. Practice it, it will be useful at some point.

SEE 5

Identify five things around you. Pay attention to them and notice the details.

TOUCH 4

Touch four things. They can be items of clothing, your phone, your desk, or a cup of tea. Any four things in your immediate vicinity that can be touched.

HEAR 3

Take note of three different sounds. This could be a bird singing, the noise coming from traffic, music from a radio or the hum of the aircon.

SMELL 2

Take a moment to pick up different scents. This could be the smell of perfume, a cup of coffee or food being cooked.

TASTE 1

Taste something. It can be a piece of gum, a soda, or food. Focus on savoring the taste of it.

CHAPTER 8

You Be You

—

"Stop comparing yourself with others. If they are good at
something you too are good at something else. Self-confidence
is not measured by your own capabilities versus that of others
but by your own needs."

—STEPHEN RICHARDS

"Am I behind in life?" my friend Sadou asked me. I didn't know how to answer the question. As she repeated herself I simply muttered, "I don't know." That was probably the best answer then, and if she were to ask me again my answer would still be the same.

I don't know about you, but just like Sadou I used to think I was behind in life. I'm not immune to that line of self-questioning. Looking at other people's lives can often give you the feeling that you're trailing behind, leading you to feel insecure. We are a generation in which social media has heightened the possibility for social comparison. Nothing is off-limits and everything is on display: job, money, status, cooking skills—the list goes on. We see Pinterest-perfect houses, Peloton-chiseled bodies and amazing runway-ready looks and we immediately feel like we don't measure up. We also have self-imposed and societal pressure that we need to be at a certain level socially, professionally and romantically by a certain age. And if we believe these ideas, we start living by an external clock. Soon enough our self-esteem is impacted, creating self-doubt and many other self-limiting beliefs.

DO YOU COMPARE YOURSELF TO OTHERS?

Comparison is judging ourselves against others and thinking that they are either better or worse than us. Whether we like it or not, we're continually evaluating ourselves against others. Comparing yourself to others could seem like a harmless activity at first. We often justify it by saying we are seeking "inspiration" and "motivation" from other people's lives, but by continually doing so, it will steal your joy and peace.

Do you identify with any of these statements? (check any that apply)

- You look at other people's lives and set your goals according to what they are doing.

- You obsess over how people perceive you, for example your social status, the job you have, who you love.

- You manipulate your online and offline image to improve your social standing.

- You feel insecure and depressed when you're around people who you think are more successful than you.

WHY DO WE DO IT?

Even though we are told to cherish our uniqueness and be comfortable in our skin, we still spend a significant amount of time comparing ourselves to others. Does that mean we're simply wired to look for pain and discontent? Why can't we stop giving our peace away?

Nearly fifty years ago, psychologist Leon Festinger came up with the social comparison theory suggesting that as humans we have a drive to evaluate ourselves in comparison to others. In short, we use reference points to figure out our place within society. Sometimes we compare ourselves to better-off people (upward comparison), or people in less favorable conditions than us (downward comparison). Upward comparison can motivate us to aim higher and stretch our abilities to improve ourselves. The downward comparison can make you feel good because at least you're not worse off than someone else. But, because of what psychologists refer to as the brain's "negative bias", we tend to be more attuned to adverse events and focus more on what we lack. For example, we're more likely to compare ourselves to the people with chiseled bodies and who run marathons than to the friends who have not stepped into the gym for years. And sooner or later we start feeling inadequate, inferior and quite miserable.

COMPARISON IS A TRAP

Comparison can offer a way to inspire and motivate oneself toward self-improvement. I'm not suggesting that you stop looking up to people who inspire you to be better in your field or in life. But because of how our brain operates, what may start as just a little bit of inspiration could turn into an obsession over what we lack and turn it into chronic comparison. But you know what? There will always be someone with a faster car, a bigger house and a better pedigree. There will always be someone who has more and is doing more. And that's okay. As author and inspirational speaker Regina Brett put it, "If we all threw our problems in a pile and saw everyone else's, we'd grab ours back." Besides ...

Having more does not equal fulfillment.
Fulfillment does not mean perfection. And
perfection does not mean happiness.

It's important not to downplay your own unique abilities. It's exhausting to cultivate the unhealthy habit of comparison, and it makes one continuously yearn for more. We have already established that as humans we're wired towards comparison, and that it could be a way to boost one's efforts and abilities. However, like everything we consume in excess, it can quickly become problematic. So, what should we do?

MORE OF YOU, LESS OF THEM

A game-changer in my life has been the adoption of the scorecard concept. I came across it via this Warren Buffett quote, "The big question about how people behave is whether they've got an inner scorecard or an outer scorecard. It helps if you can be satisfied with an inner scorecard."

An inner scorecard is an internal compass that directs what we seek to achieve—our goals—and what we decide to entertain. We don't let others be the judge of our performance. On the other hand, with an outer scorecard, the emphasis is on how we are perceived in comparison to others and how the world views us. It's normal to care about how other people view us but it shouldn't be to our detriment.

The woman or man you see in the mirror every day is the one you will have to live with for the rest of your life. Only you know the goals, the dreams and the things you have set out to accomplish. Only then will you be able to measure if you are improving or not, and if you are a better version of yourself today than you were yesterday. So, the only way not to be left behind in your life is to focus on all you have already accomplished. If you genuinely think you have not accomplished anything yet, get busy building that inner scorecard.

You are on your journey

Contrary to what people like to say, it's not you against the world. It's you against you! Your talents and skills are yours. You have them because they are contributions you can make to the world. It's all well and good to be inspired and learn from people who have taken the journey before us. But mainly, we despair over the comparisons we make with others. Would you be upset if we met at the airport and you were going to Peru and I was going to Papua New Guinea and I got to my destination before you? I bet you wouldn't because you'd understand that our destinations are different, and so the time it took each of us to get there would be different too.

Comparing yourself to others means that you are busy peeking into someone else's life rather than focusing on your own. We worry over someone that's reached chapter 99 in their book of life while we're still busy with our first chapter. In the wise words of football coach Sven Goran Eriksson, "To wish you were someone else is to waste the person you are."

EMBRACE AN ABUNDANCE MINDSET

Every time I found myself obsessing over other people's lives and the things they did, I realized that I had lost sight of my own goals and mission. When we let comparison rent space in our minds we start becoming filled with doubt, opening the door to a scarcity mentality. We begin to think that there's not enough in the world for all of us. Cultivating an abundance mindset means that we embrace the fact that there's plenty of resources out there for everyone. Someone else's success and progress shouldn't hold you back from doing the same or even better. Adopting this mindset enables you to focus on watering the garden in your own life instead of comparing, envying, resenting or coveting someone else's progress.

Consider the following suggestions to help you avoid comparing yourself to others:

BRAVER

IN ACTION: AVOID COMPARISON	
Instead of:	**Consider this:**
Focusing on where others are in their progress.	**Shift the focus back to you.** Develop your inner scorecard by comparing yourself to where you were last year or five years ago etc.
Expressing negative emotions and contempt over your life.	**Practice gratitude.** You may not be where you want to be but you are not where you once were. Find one to three things daily that you are grateful for. Write it down or say it out aloud.
Obsessing over what's missing in your life.	**Do something for someone else.** Taking the focus off your life and doing something for someone else will help you put life into perspective.
Being triggered by what you see on social media.	**Remember** that most people only show their best lives on social media. It is barely reality. Make sure that you do a social media fast from time to time.

89

BRAVER STORY

With

EMILY BLUNT

Who knew that the world-famous actress Emily Blunt battled with stuttering? Did you know that the speech disorder was a catalyst to her success?

British-born Emily Blunt burst onto our screens with her astounding performance in 2006's *Devil Wears Prada*, going on to establish a remarkable career for herself. So it might be surprising for people to hear that she had battled with a debilitating stutter growing up. Interestingly, through her stuttering, she found her voice and ignited her love for theater.

When she was still in grade school, one of her teachers suggested that she try out for the school play. While initially horrified by the idea, she gave it a try and to her shock she was able to deliver her lines correctly without any stuttering. As she put it herself, to deal with the stutter she developed a talent for talking in a "lot of funny voices because I could speak more fluently if I didn't sound like me."

Emily Blunt went on to become an award-winning actress and a global icon. In her interviews, she made it clear that she was constantly bullied as a child for being different when all she wanted was to be like everyone else and be heard. Now she's being heard and seen by audiences all around the world. Blunt focused on turning her speech impediment into something positive instead of comparing herself to other people. The lesson is this: you can turn a loss into a win by focusing on your unique journey. Always.

A BRAVER YOU

In Action

DEVELOP YOUR INNER SCORECARD

If you want to get more out of your life, you will only achieve it by changing your mindset from outward to inward. Cue your inner scorecard.

The inner scorecard is all about deciding what's important to you. You'll measure your life according to the criteria you set for yourself and not in comparison to others. Having an inner scorecard gives you a reference point for when you're confronted with difficult choices. It can also give you more clarity. Because this is another value-based exercise, I strongly recommend that you go back to Chapter 2 if you skipped it. For everyone else, come through. Let's get this started!

We will build our inner scorecard with key performance indicators (KPIs) like in a work performance review, except this will be way more fun. For this exercise, we'll use some questions in different categories for initial reflection. So:

1. Get started by asking yourself questions using the "Am I ___ " in different categories in your life. You can create your questions however you like. The goal is to get you thinking. Examples:

   - *Personal*: Am I open to new growth and am I investing enough in my development? Am I committed to my purpose?

   - *Social*: Am I happy with my relationships and friendships?

   - *Health:* Am I leading a healthy lifestyle?

   - *Career*: Am I pursuing a job that's aligned with my skills? Am I being challenged enough?

2. Create your metrics in different categories. For example, your career metric could have you being bolder next year and applying for a very senior position.

3. Come back to grade yourself once the time you have set has lapsed. You could do your review every three, six or twelve months—it's up to you.

4. Evaluate your performance by giving it a grade. For those areas where you are not performing well, identify actionable next steps you can take to improve.

5. Apply and live by your inner scorecard.

CHAPTER 9

Let It Go

—

"Forgiveness isn't approving what happened.

It's choosing to rise above it."

—ROBIN SHARMA

I was packing boxes in my childhood home when I came across it: my math book from the 10th grade. I thought my parents had gotten rid of all of our early schooling files. Out of all of the books I could find, I had to find *that* one.

It's strange how the sight of a tiny object could bring about so much emotion and a flood of bad memories. As I was coming out of my stupor I turned to my sister, Nadiath, who was also busy sorting through her own set of boxes:

"Do you remember Mr. LeCon?" I asked while still staring at the maths book.

"Hmm ... who?" asked Nadiath.

"My math professor in 10th grade," I replied.

"Oh! That funny guy with the mustache and the oversized biceps?" she said while bursting out laughing. "What about him?"

"I hate that guy. The way he used to tell me that I would amount to nothing because I was always failing the math tests? He made me feel like crap and so scared of failure."

"Wait ... stop. What?" She stopped and turned towards me and laughed. "You are still thinking about Mr. LeCon? It's been almost fifteen years! Why are you even allowing that guy to rent space in your head? Girl, you know he ain't thinking about you.

That guy was—and probably still is—mean to so many people. Let it go. Forgive."

Let it go? Forgive? It's not like I was holding onto a grudge. Or was I? Okay, okay, maybe I was. It's not like I hadn't tried. I had written in my journal and talked about it at great lengths with friends and family, most of the time they just laughed it off. I've heard countless times that holding onto anger, hatred and pain is not healthy and moving on is essential. But at various times I felt stuck in 10th grade in that advanced maths class. I could vividly see myself seated at my desk, just behind my friend Anoko. I would try to hide behind her bouncy afro, hoping he wouldn't ask me to answer one of those gibberish questions. Either that or he would humiliate me by revealing that I received the lowest grade on the exam *again*.

I have gone on to get various degrees over the years. I even got one in finance just to prove to myself that I wasn't innumerate. I might not have made it to Wall Street but I framed that degree on my wall and it's a great ego booster. I should scan it and send it to Mr. LeCon. I wish I had his address! I thought doing so would put all these horrible memories and feelings of inadequacy to rest. But why was I still ruminating over something that happened ages ago? Forgiveness ...

DO YOU STRUGGLE TO FORGIVE?

But first, what is forgiveness? Psychologists define forgiveness as the mental process of ceasing to feel resentment, anger and vengeance against another person who may have hurt us.

Can you relate to any of these?

- You continue to dwell on the situation and the hurt.
- You want "payback" and are looking for opportunities for revenge.
- You have no peace and only think of negative thoughts when you think of the situation and the person.
- You still talk disparagingly about the people who hurt you.

WHY DO WE STRUGGLE TO FORGIVE?

"God may forgive your sins, but your nervous system won't."
—ALFRED KORZYBSKI

Research has shown that we tend to ruminate more about adverse events than positive ones because those pesky negative events require more thinking. That kind of information is processed more thoroughly by our brain. So, there it is! It is our brain's fault. That's how we are wired—end of the story. But that doesn't mean we should accept being stuck in the past. We can't just walk away without taking any responsibility. In my own experience, I think there is a part of me that may have enjoyed being stuck in the past. Waking up every day and having someone to blame, reliving the mistreatment and cursing the hell out of him in my head was somehow soothing. I mean, who doesn't want a villain in their lives, right? Obsessing over how I was treated—even if it was more than a decade ago—gave me ammunition to feel sad and wallow in plenty of self-pity. But the more I replayed those awful high school situations in my head, the more I couldn't move forward.

We struggle to forgive because sometimes we want to sweep everything under the rug and forget about it. Some people even go as far as to say "forgive and forget" to inspire us to quickly move forward. While this advice is well-meaning, you can forgive a situation and still remember it. The issue hits home every time we think about a past situation. We still harbor negative feelings, stress and grudges that we carry into our present. Did I forgive overnight? No. Did it take me some time? Yes. Forgiveness requires time, patience and courage. But more importantly, it's a decision.

GETTING RID OF THE POISON

Professor Robert Enright, a pioneer in the scientific study of forgiveness, believes that forgiveness is a conscious decision to be fair to people who were not good to you. A mental decision to release, to grow, to go forward. A mental decision to see the poison alert and to stop drinking from the unforgiveness bottle. Bad things are bound to happen, even if you are a fantastic person. We are bound to disappoint and be disappointed. In our lifetime we will likely get hurt and perhaps even hurt others. That's life. And if we hold onto the hurt and all the unhealthy emotions it will only hold us back emotionally, mentally and physically.

Forgiveness is about you and for you.

You may have been stuck agonizing over that failed relationship, a work presentation gone wrong, a betrayal from a friend, or some devastating life event. In each case, there is no magic pill or formula that any of us can take to release the pain, shame or anger from any situation. Whatever place you find yourself in, whatever your reason, not being able to forgive is like carrying a millstone around your neck. It will stop you from moving forward with your life.

Now, forgiveness does not mean pretending that the situation never happened or letting people who may have harmed you back into your life. Far from that. You owe it to yourself to protect your energy, your space and your life. Setting yourself free and moving to a place of forgiveness will sometimes require that you first forgive yourself. In my case, self-forgiveness was letting go of what I thought I should have done differently. All those times I blamed myself for not standing up for myself or for not studying harder. To forgive myself, I needed to release the negative emotions associated with that experience. In my mind Mr. LeCon was not deserving of it but it did not matter. By forgiving him I released the negative emotions and replaced them with ones that helped me embrace life's beauty and joy.

THE ROAD TO FORGIVENESS

Forgiveness is the freedom to choose who and what you allow to rent space in your head. You may think that you're in control when harboring resentment in your heart but the truth is you have given your power away.

Think about it.

IN ACTION: FORGIVENESS	
Instead of:	**Consider this:**
Dwelling on the past and the hurt.	**Address the pain**. Who hurt you and how? The starting point is to first do an audit of where your hurt is coming from before you can take steps to forgive.
Looking for ways to take revenge.	We talked earlier about compassion. **Think about extending compassion** to someone who may have hurt you. Look at them as someone who is just like you and makes mistakes too. It's not about excusing the actions of the person, it's about developing empathy to make it easier to forgive.

BRAVER TIP

By

EVERETT WORTHINGTON

Forgiveness is a choice. And while it's not always easy, it's necessary. Everett Worthington, a clinical psychologist, developed the REACH forgiveness model—a five-step process to practicing forgiveness. Here's how it works:

1. **Recall the hurt**

   First and foremost, you need to recognize that you have been hurt and are still dealing with the pain.

2. **Empathize**

   Put yourself in that person's shoes. Try to understand, without judging, why the person who hurt you may have acted in that way.

3. **Altruistic gift**

   Consider forgiveness as an altruistic gift. We've all hurt someone at some point in our life but we have also been given the gift of forgiveness.

4. **Commit**

   Forgiveness is a commitment. Once you have forgiven someone else, you need to encourage yourself to stay in the "forgiveness zone".

5. **Hold**

   Stay in the forgiveness zone. Remind yourself that you have already practiced forgiveness and trust that it's done.

A BRAVER YOU

In Action

FORGIVENESS LETTER

If there's someone in your life, past or present, you need to forgive, consider writing them a forgiveness letter. A forgiveness letter is an opportunity for you to offload the hurt, disappointment and anger you may still harbor against this person. A forgiveness letter is a positive step towards peace, healing and control over a situation that makes you feel helpless. The letter may not eradicate the hurt overnight, but it will allow you to pour out your thoughts and feelings about everything that transpired between the two of you in a non-judgmental way. Here's what you'll need:

1. A quiet space where you can sit still without any interruptions so that you can gather your thoughts.

2. A pen or pencil and a piece of paper.

I've provided a template that you can use as a starting point but feel free to create your own one. Steps to take:

STEP 1:

Before writing the letter, think through what happened (the who, the what and the where).

STEP 2:

Write the letter.

STEP 3:

Some people, like me, find it cathartic to burn, shred or trash the letter. What you do with it is up to you. The key is to put your feelings down on paper to let go of the pain and heal.

100

FORGIVENESS LETTER

Who hurt me? (talk about the person here)

_____

_____

_____

_____

_____

What actions did the person take that hurt me?

_____

_____

_____

_____

What emotions do I feel about the person?

_____

_____

_____

_____

Based on the above, formulate your letter below:

_____

_____

_____

_____

_____

_____

_____

_____

_____

CHAPTER 10

Find Your Magic

—

"A comfort zone is a beautiful place,

but nothing ever grows there."

—JOHN ASSARAF

It was a dream.

A dream we could finally scratch off our bucket list—an all-girls trip to Punta Cana, Dominican Republic. We had worked eight odd jobs between the five of us, ungodly long hours and saved all our pennies for this idyllic Caribbean vacation. Pristine white beaches, warm waters and lazy days sipping pina coladas and eating delicious *tostones* (fried Dominican plantains) were just what we dreamed of. But beyond the all-inclusive appeal, we picked Punta Cana for the thrill of adventure and the exhilarating activities on offer, from sailing and zip-lining to snorkeling. We wanted to experience everything!

It looked so fancy and so foreign, so we made a point to add it to our "Thrill List." The Thrill List was self-explanatory: we would only undertake activities that would take us out of our comfort zones. We wanted to push the boundaries of what we could do and attempt things we hadn't done before. The whole trip to Punta Cana was already out of our wallet zone, so we might as well go all out. And all out we went ... into the sea.

When our boat for the snorkeling activity stopped in the middle of the sea, we glanced at each other with worried looks on our faces. Unperturbed, our guide and boat operator started handing out the necessary gear. Fins, wetsuits and so on were being passed around, leaving us more and more puzzled. Eventually, I broke the silence. "I'm not doing this. I don't know how to swim," I exclaimed. The other girls burst out laughing and were all like, "This is not what we imagined. Can we please go back to shore?" The instructor was speechless and stared at us. He was probably thinking that we were joking. "What kind of idiots go snorkeling when they don't even know how to swim?" So back to the shore we went.

Looking back, this was an extreme case of stepping out of a comfort zone. It could have ended in tragedy considering that we didn't know how to swim. While our first attempt at snorkeling didn't pan out as expected, it did motivate us to learn how to swim. Some of us in the group eventually did end up going snorkeling after all. The lesson in this story: just because we stretched ourselves and wanted to do something different did not mean we would succeed at first. The most important thing was our willingness to step out of our comfort zone.

THE COMFORT ZONE

"I learned to always take on things I had never done before. Growth and comfort do not coexist.

—VIRGINIA ROMETTY

You hear it a lot: step out of your comfort zone. Your friends and family talk about it. Magazine columnists and career coaches advocate for it. We all have a comfort zone—a cozy cocoon, our kingdom and the bubble from where we operate. It's safe, familiar and where our routines live. This is the zone where we feel comfortable, calm and where we have control. This love for control stops us from seeing the world in a new way and going after what we truly deserve. Sometimes we don't even know that we are in a comfort zone. We get so accustomed to the familiar, even when it no longer serves us, that it's hard to see beyond our self-induced fog.

So, are you currently inside or outside of your comfort zone? See how many of these statements apply to you:

- Your life is predictable, the same old thing just a different day.

- You are not learning anything new.

- You are frustrated with your life and you let things happen to you.

- You can't remember the last time you tried something new.

- You are afraid of rejection so you settle with what you have.

WHY WE GET STUCK IN THE COMFORT ZONE

Many of us learn to stay in our comfort zone early on in life. As children, we're told to stop asking so many questions. We're advised to get good grades, to pursue a college degree, to get a good job and voila! Stay within those parameters and you've made it. No wonder we get so comfortable. This box we've created for ourselves is the promised land—the place where milk and honey abound. Beyond that, we're also afraid of the unknown. As our brain evaluates the cost-benefit of taking risks and stepping out with purpose, we tend to focus on everything that could go wrong before thinking about what could go right. Our comfort zone is especially appealing when we battle with self-doubt. When we doubt our ability to accomplish our dreams, we end up procrastinating. In the end, we lose out on opportunities and keep making excuses about why we are living a mediocre life when we are deserving of so much more.

DISTURBING YOUR COMFORT ZONE

We sometimes look at other people's lives, the famous and not so famous, and wonder how and why they are so successful. Everyone else seems to be thriving and living up to their full potential while we feel stuck in places and situations that look the same year after year. I'm sure their success has a lot to do with discipline, commitment and hard work, but they also had to leap out of their comfort zone. Getting out of our comfort zone is uncomfortable. It's about intentionally relinquishing control. Many of us are so used to our lives being predictable. We take the same route to work, we know where our favorite burger joint is, we run in the same park. We have our routines, and yes, we would like to stick with them. But it has been said that everything we ever want resides outside of our comfort zone.

To get the most out of life you must move forward, and to do so you have to take action. There's no growth in doing the same thing over and over again. Doing the same thing and expecting different results is, according to Albert Einstein, the definition of insanity. You are not insane, are you? Stepping out of your comfort zone doesn't mean you have to make life-altering changes that cause you anxiety or stress. I'm not saying you should try snorkeling (with no swimming skills) or go bungee jumping or attempt a triathlon—unless that's your thing. It's not about doing dramatic and outlandish things. The point is to start looking critically at your daily habits so that you can step outside the circle you've formed around them. It's about making small changes that get you out of your rut without making you anxious. It could be as small and as simple as taking a new route to work (who knows what new places you could discover on the way), trying a new coffee shop, reading a different type of magazine or book, or taking on an activity that may be a bit unusual for you.

BE SCARED BUT DO IT ANYWAY

It's scary to step out of your comfort zone but it's doable. You know a change needs to take place and you are waiting for it. Sorry friend, it won't come until you implement it.

Seeking change is good.

Actioning change is even better.

You are the change you are waiting for. Instead of waiting for someone to come and hold your hand, you will have to make the leap yourself. Here are a couple of things you can do to help you get out of your comfort zone:

IN ACTION: STEP OUT OF YOUR COMFORT ZONE	
Instead of:	**Consider this:**
Feeling frustrated and letting life pass you by.	**Decide which areas of your life** you want to change. Pick one area and focus on it to get started, then move on to the others.
Talking yourself out of what's possible.	**Change your self-talk.** The stories you tell yourself matter. Start telling yourself that what you want is possible. Your self-talk has power so use it wisely and to your benefit.
Being bored with your life and wanting to live someone else's life.	**Take small steps in** one specific area to get out of your comfort zone. Start where you are and with what you have.

BRAVER STORY

With

SHONDA RHIMES

If you're familiar with American TV shows, you would have by now come across Shonda Rhimes' brilliant and groundbreaking work. Think *Grey's Anatomy*, *Scandal* and *How to Get Away with Murder*. They've all been created by Rhimes.

A mega-talented executive producer, Shonda Rhimes has taken over American television in the past decade. But while she was soaring professionally, she was miserable. Rhimes had gotten into the habit of saying "no" to anything that would take her away from her home. She loathed public appearances, media interviews and social events, preferring to stay home and work. That was until her sister told her during a thanksgiving dinner, "You never say yes to anything."

Those six words were a wake-up call and made Rhimes realize that she needed a change. She was using the excuse of being "busy" to hide the truth: she was afraid to step out of her comfort zone. So Rhimes committed herself to one year of saying "yes" to everything from commencement speeches and social events, to accepting more help—and finally saying yes to herself.

Committing herself to say yes for a year not only helped her to confront her fears and get out of her comfort zone, but it also significantly changed her life in the process.

What about you? What do you need to say YES to?

A BRAVER YOU

In Action

YOUR PATH TO YES

As with the story of Shonda Rhimes, no one is immune to the warm cocoon that is the comfort zone. For our *In Action* exercise today, we are going to get out of our comfort zones. So:

STEP ONE:

Pick one category in your life that needs to be switched up: professional, social, romantic etc.

STEP TWO:

Pick one area within the category that you want to focus on. For example, within the social type, the focus may be on speaking to strangers at events.

STEP THREE:

Write at least one goal related to the area you want to change. You can do as many as three if you like. Your goal needs to specify the "who" (you), the "what" (activities/actions you'll take), the "when" (by which date) and the "where" (the exact place where actions will be taken). An example of a focused goal may be that you will speak for at least five minutes to a stranger on your train ride tomorrow. Done!

STEP FOUR:

Take your goal and action it. You can stare at a written goal all you want, but unless you activate it, nothing will happen.

You can repeat the process to get out of your comfort zone in as many categories of your life as you like. As I like to say, "Focus is better than speed." Start small and smash one comfort zone at a time.

BOLDER

// To be courageous or daring

—

Well done — you've made it past the first two weeks!

We've worked through your limiting limits, took stock of where you are and uncovered the values that matter most to you. Yet we've still got so many inroads to make.

The next chapter of your journey is all about embracing self-care, crushing your fears, developing sustainable daily rituals, beating procrastination and building discipline.

Enough said. Let's carry on, shall we?

CHAPTER 11

Self-Care Matters

—

"Self-care is giving the world the best of you, instead of what's left of you."

—KATIE REED

It was 6:30 p.m. and I was walking to my twice-weekly therapy session. I usually went for mid-day sessions but since walk-ins were also welcome I knew there was nothing to worry about.

This was no ordinary therapy session though. There was no checking-in with a receptionist, no initial paperwork to fill out and there was a diverse range of therapists to choose from to treat an array of psychological issues. I had been coming here for a while, and even though my mental and emotional problems had yet to disappear, I felt heard and seen. My therapist's office was in between two old, crusty buildings in the northern suburb of Evanston in Chicago. The space was a very unassuming small building with yellow signage and bright blue paint. There was usually a queue outside the building for walk-ins but the wait was worth it. Today, though, there was no queue as I proceeded directly to the counter and asked for my preferred therapist— Cajun fries with a double load of melted cheddar cheese and jalapeno chilies! The buttery mix of paprika and cayenne pepper had a way of giving me all the feels.

As I said, this was no ordinary therapy.

I used fries to cure my emotional needs and find comfort. Just like I used pizza for stress relief. Just like I reached for energy drinks to deal with my lethargy. As you can imagine, my diet was a mess and my energy was at an all-time low. And the less energy I had, the more caffeinated beverages I consumed. It was a vicious cycle but I repeatedly justified it by reminding myself that I deserved to do whatever I wanted and eat whatever I wanted. "You are working so hard! You deserve to make yourself happy from time to time." But the "from time to time" became all the time. And before long, I had unofficial subscriptions to fast food places across the city. "It's self-care," I rationalized. "It is not that bad. Everyone does it." But was it self-care?

WHAT IS SELF-CARE?

Self-care is a broad concept that is more mainstream now than ever before. It may mean different things to different people but self-care is not about being indulgent or selfish. Self-care is not about numbing yourself with so-called "feel good" things like excessive drinking and overeating. Effective self-care is a series of actions and activities you engage in to take care of your physical, mental and emotional health. Effective self-care is all about long-term benefits instead of short-term relief. Embracing self-care will help you reap considerable benefits.

WHY WE NEGLECT SELF-CARE?

Do any of these sound familiar?

- You are often moody, have low energy and feel stressed out.

- You have lost touch with yourself and your goals.

- You don't feel like yourself anymore.

- You berate yourself for the smallest mistakes.

- Your priorities are at the bottom of your to-do list.

- You put other people first and barely have time for the things you want to do.

- You feel isolated.

If you see yourself in any of the points above, you are not alone. Many of us struggle with prioritizing and making time for self-care. Some of the reasons for this could be:

The time factor: a lot of us claim that we simply don't have time for self-care. There's too much to do and it's just not possible to make time for it. But that's not entirely true. We tend to make time for things we value. It's not so much the "having the time" for self-care, it is all about "making the time" for self-care.

Numbing is not self-care: sometimes we confuse numbing ourselves with the practice of self-care. By overindulging on fast food, I thought I was practicing self-care. But in reality it was just a coping mechanism to mask the pain from the isolation permeating my life.

Professional guidance: self-care is also recognizing when you need to reach out for professional help. Sometimes it's just not possible to "DIY".

Maybe your self-care needs are around taking better care of your body and you might need a fitness trainer or a specialized masseuse. In my experience, I needed to reach out to a mental health professional. The more I numbed my pain with temporary fixes, the more my mental health deteriorated. I had trouble sleeping, and couldn't focus in class or at work. This was combined with hysterical crying episodes in the toilets in between classes or sometimes even at the office. All the fries and juicy steaks of the world could not sort it out. Nothing was getting better and I was buying myself time but not solving the issue. The only way I could get better was when I finally reached out for help and got counseling at the campus clinic.

We often avoid bringing specialists into our lives for fear of how we will be perceived or what people will say. But we need to start leaving the superheroes to the movie industry! There's nothing wrong with asking for help, reaching out to others and taking guidance from people who have the knowledge and experience to help you.

STEP UP YOUR SELF-CARE GAME

If you want to live a fulfilled life, you have to take care of your body and mind. It's as important (if not more so) as your daughter's ballet recital or those extra hours you're putting in at work to finish a project. You won't be of use to anyone if you don't prioritize your physical, emotional and mental needs. Self-care is an individual practice and I like to use the oxygen mask analogy on the plane as an example. When you board a plane, they give you instructions that you need to put on your oxygen mask first before helping anyone else around you in case of an emergency. That advice is golden because caring for others starts with caring for yourself. What's the point of burning out at work or putting in all those extra hours towards your side-hustle if you have nothing left over for yourself?

Self-care is not a luxury, it's a priority.

What airlines are trying to tell us is that we ought to be taking care of our well-being first. That's the real first class! Except you get to customize your self-care package, it's not a one-size-fits-all approach. Your needs are different from mine so only you know what's best for you. If you're ready to upgrade your life and your self-care game, take a look at these suggestions:

IN ACTION: STEP UP YOUR SELF-CARE GAME	
Instead of:	**Consider this:**
Looking at what others are doing and copying their self-care routines.	**Identify your self-care needs.** Which areas of your life do you need to prioritize? Physical, mental or emotional. Write down your needs in each category.
Trying different things on a whim.	For each category, **determine the practice** you would like to adopt. Stick to one and do it.
Trying to do everything at the same time.	**Monitor your experience** with the practice. Replace the practice as needed.

SELF-CARE

1
PHYSICAL

Think about the activities that will improve your physical well-being (eat healthily, exercise regularly, get enough sleep, etc.

2
EMOTIONAL

Think about the activities that will bring about more awareness of your feelings (going for therapy, journaling, etc.)

SOCIAL
3

Think about activities that will improve the relationships in your life (spend more time with friends and family etc.)

SPIRITUAL
4

Think about activities that will nurture your spirit and soul (spend time alone, meditate, prayers, walk in nature, etc.)

MENTAL
5

Think about activities that will stimulate your intellect (reading a good book, learning a new skill, finding a mentor etc.)

PRACTICAL
6

Think about the things you can do now to minimize future stressors in your life. (create a weekly budget, declutter your house, find your routine, sign up for a life insurance policy, etc.)

A BOLDER YOU

In Action

YOUR SELF-CARE ROUTINE

Right, time to build your self-care routine! Remember, this is personal and there's no perfect plan. The one you will get to design and action is the only one that will be perfect for you.

1. **Use the layout** provided in the next page or create your own.

2. **Fill your self-care plan with activities** that you'll enjoy. For a start, I suggest sticking to one activity in each category. You can always switch it up if you don't like it down the line.

3. **Make sure it's visible.** Put it somewhere where you can see it, and make sure that you share it with your accountability partners. The most crucial part is that you engage in those activities you've selected.

4. **Evaluate your plan every 30 days or so** to see if it's still working for you. Nothing is set in stone, so you can make adjustments any time that you want to. The main thing is that you are making progress towards your well-being.

SELF-CARE PLAN

CURRENT PRACTICES
Here are the practices I currently have:

EMOTIONALLY

- ☐
- ☐

MENTALLY

- ☐
- ☐

PRACTICALLY

- ☐
- ☐

SPIRITUALLY

- ☐
- ☐

SOCIALLY

- ☐
- ☐

PHYSICALLY

- ☐
- ☐

NEW PRACTICES
Here are the practices I want to explore:

EMOTIONALLY

- ☐
- ☐

MENTALLY

- ☐
- ☐

PRACTICALLY

- ☐
- ☐

SPIRITUALLY

- ☐
- ☐

SOCIALLY

- ☐
- ☐

PHYSICALLY

- ☐
- ☐

1. What support to need to implement these practices?

_____

2. Who can I rely on for these practices?

_____

CHAPTER 12

Fear Is The Fuel

—

"Your destiny is too great, your assignment too

important, your time too valuable. Do not let fear

intimidate you."

—JOEL OSTEEN

Have you ever had a friend who seemed to have your best interests at heart but also held you back from living your best life?

Friendship is about mutual respect, affection and genuinely wanting the best for the other person. It's about being around people who will lift you and help you make better life choices. It's your friends that hold you up in tough times when you need support the most. Tiny was all of the above—at first. I can't remember when Tiny and I first became friends. She had seemed to be a constant part of my life for a long time, and she was just like a family member.

Her name may have been Tiny, but she was powerful, strong-willed and bold. So much so that I frequently yielded to her advice as it had always felt that she was looking out for my best interests and trying to keep me out of harm's way. I gave her my undivided attention and followed through with her advice. But there were also unhealthy elements to our friendship. Every time I wanted to attempt something new, she would hold me back. Each time her voice became louder and more imposing, and she would throw dart after dart of scolding, shaming and fault-finding.

Her preferred choice of words were, "you are useless," "you don't have the experience" and "you will make a joke of yourself". For the longest time I believed her even though I disapproved of her harsh words. But I rationalized it by telling myself that she knew me best and was looking out for me and my best interests. But was she *really* though? In reality, she was keeping me small. She would always dwell on my past mistakes, bring up the worst possible scenarios and replay tapes from my past frustrations and negative life experiences. She would champion all of these into a rousing speech on why I couldn't do anything more than what I was already doing.

I can't pinpoint when I realized the friendship kept me stuck in "Fear Town," but I eventually gathered that if I kept listening to Tiny, I would never live up to my potential and soar personally or professionally. But Tiny was not the kind of friend you could easily ghost and remove from your life. Where would I find a manual on how to break up with the voice in my head? Yes, Tiny was in my head. She was *the* fear standing between me and my next move, but I had finally decided that I was not going to let her win.

UNDERSTANDING FEAR

When talking about fear, we immediately assume that it's a bad thing and an emotion that should be avoided at all costs. The standard narrative states that if you're fearful, then you're weak. We're constantly reminded that in order to achieve our goals, we need to rise above our fears.

But that's not true.

Fear seeks to protect: it's not our enemy and it has its place. Experiencing fear is embedded in our nature and is essential to our survival. As psychologists explain it, fear has good intentions. It's there to help us stay alert, cope and steer us through situations that could be dangerous, overwhelming or worth paying attention to—basically, to shield us from harm.

Fear seeks to teach: it will show us what we should avoid. Fear can be our guide in showing us how to behave and adjust. If we could not feel fear, we would probably all be dead by now! Think about it: if we had no fear whatsoever, we would be putting ourselves in the line of unimaginable danger which could result in death. But if fear is so positive, why does it get such a bad rap?

TWO SIDES OF THE SAME COIN

We all know that anything that is consumed without moderation can quickly become detrimental. For example, working out is great for our bodies but if we overdo it we could get injured. I like to think about fear in the same way. Fear has two sides: the good kind that is helpful, intuitive and wants the best for you. Then you have the bad kind that stops you from living your life to the fullest. It's this kind of bad fear that we need to be mindful of if we are to make real progress in our lives.

You are consumed with bad fear if:

- You are scared of going after your dreams.

- You hesitate to try new things because you only see obstacles, not opportunities.

- You are always thinking about what could go wrong instead of what could go right.

- You seek perfection before attempting anything new.

- You are continually planning things but never actually getting around to doing them.

Fear exists to protect you from others, nature and sometimes even from yourself. But if left to run wild, fear has the potential to be debilitating. It could prevent you from doing anything enjoyable and stop you from going after your dreams. For you to thrive and live up to your full potential, you'll have to learn to recognize the differences between good and bad fear. You'll also need to learn how to manage them effectively as both can manifest in the same way: increased heart rate, difficulty breathing, tight sensation in your chest and nausea. From a physical perspective, it can be hard to differentiate between the two but I remind myself of their differences in the following way:

126

Bad fear restrains you from taking action.

Good fear empowers you to take action.

FEARLESSNESS IS NOT A THING

Allow me to repeat this: the presence of courage doesn't mean the absence of fear. You can still be scared but take the necessary steps to do what you have to do. Unfortunately, we are constantly reminded that it's only when we become fearless that our life will become limitless, and that being fearless is our secret weapon. I get it. All of these statements and quotations exist to keep us motivated. But deep down they also spread a false philosophy—that we ought to be utterly fearless to achieve anything worthwhile in our lives. Well, I guess I must have failed at life then because I'm not fearless. If I needed to get rid of all my fears before writing this book, I wouldn't have done it at all! I was terrified when I wrote this book, even more so now that you are reading it. For those still tracking with me, I decided not to let fear scare and stop me. I took small steps to do what I set out to do despite my worries.

I don't know anyone who is not afraid of something. The most successful people I know and admire all have fears. Some fear failure, death or any number of other anxieties. But they keep going and don't let their fears deter them from going forward and smashing their goals. And that's why I have redefined what "fearless" means to me. When I think about being fearless, I don't think about the lack of fear. I see it as looking boldly into fear and doing what I have to do anyway.

Being fearless is not about faking it through your fears
or not having fear. Real fearlessness is about not letting
fear make decisions for you. It's about not giving in and
pushing through.

127

When you feel fear, you have to choose to not let it consume you. Fear sends us signals and the way we react to these signals is our choice. Fear will invite itself to your party anytime you step out and try to do something new or uncomfortable. It's up to you to decide not to let it ruin your party. You'll pay a high price if you let fear take over your life. You'll be unhappy, moody and continuously feel as though you're wasting away, stuck in a life that no longer pleases you. Letting fear run amok in your life is dangerous. So, be afraid, and do it anyway. The only way you can overcome fear is to face it, to take action by not letting fear make decisions for you.

OVERCOMING THE BAD FEAR

When faced with a dose of bad fear, feel it and face it head-on. When you have acknowledged the presence of the fear, you will summon all the courage you need to handle it.

Here are a few tips to help you the next time bad fears show up:

IN ACTION: TAKING A STAND AGAINST BAD FEARS	
Instead of:	**Consider this:**
Entertaining unhelpful thoughts and the fear of what might go wrong.	**Identify and face the fear(s) head on by writing it down.** Having them on paper will help you realize that they aren't as scary as they seem. We talk about all the steps to follow in the *In Action* exercise for the day.
Being afraid of attempting new things and convincing yourself that you will make a joke of yourself.	**Allow your curiosity to take over.** Tell yourself instead that you are going to look into these things and see what's possible.
Trying to do everything at the same time.	**Imagine fear as a separate person in your mind.** Give it a persona so it can help you visualize the interactions as if you were talking to a friend. This is what I did by naming my fear "Tiny."

BOLDER TIP

With

SUSAN JEFFERS

I absolutely love Susan Jeffers' philosophy on fear. The renowned psychologist and author has spent a lifetime analyzing fear. I have adopted her approach as a mantra, and every time I recite it, I replace the "you" with "I" to make it more personal.

FEAR TRUTH #1

The fear will never go away as long as you continue to grow!

FEAR TRUTH #2

The only way to get rid of the fear of doing something is to go out and ... do it!

FEAR TRUTH #3

The only way to feel better about yourself is to go out and ... do it!

FEAR TRUTH #4

Not only are you afraid when facing the unknown, so is everyone else!

FEAR TRUTH #5

Pushing through fear is less frightening than living with the bigger underlying fear that comes from a feeling of helplessness.

A BOLDER YOU

In Action

BUILD YOUR FEAR LADDER

While it's normal to want to avoid the things you fear, you'll only overcome them if you face up to them. Today, our *In Action* exercise is focused on creating a fear ladder. A fear ladder involves making a list of situations you fear and ranking them from the least scary to the scariest. You'll also commit to taking steps towards eradicating them. Let's go!

Here's what you'll need:

- **Grab some paper and a pen or pencil** (I hope you haven't run out of stationery, we still have some way to go ☺).

- **Think of something you are afraid to do**—only one thing for now.

- **Set a specific goal for that fear.** What would you like to do? When and where do you want to do it? How often would you like to do it? Be specific.

- **Think of at least five activities** related to that goal. Build a list of steps that can help you work towards your goal.

- **Rank how difficult each step** is on a 0-10 scale and arrange the steps from the easiest to the hardest. Now for the fun part! Commit to tackling each one. Today, tomorrow or next week, it's your call. Start by trying the easiest step first.

- **Reward yourself** every time you tick one of the steps off your list. I've created a template below that you can adopt if you like. I've also included an example of my version in the resources section at the end of the book.

MY FEAR LADDER

Date:

What I am afraid of ? (Focus on one specific fear only)

What is my goal?

1 - 2 - 3 - 4 - 5 - 6 - 7 - 8 - 9 - 10
No Fear   Moderate Fear   Extreme Fear

Activity	Fear rating

I will attempt the following activities (List the above from easiest to hardest)

1. ....
2. ....
3. ....
4. ....
5. ....

CHAPTER 13

The Power Of Rituals

—

"A daily ritual is a way of saying, I am voting for myself,

I am taking care of myself."

—MARIEL HEMINGWAY

Ritual. When you think of the word "ritual" what comes to mind? Did you imagine a prayer, people in a circle chanting or perhaps meditation? Did you think about a religious setting? Or maybe a traditional event?

You're not wrong. Webster's dictionary defines a *ritual* as "a formal ceremony or series of acts that is always performed in the same way." Countless rituals have been in place since the beginning of humankind. You're probably more familiar with the religious kind. Think, for example, of the Holy Communion in Christianity or the six prayers a day in Islam—the list goes on. But rituals are not just performed in religious settings or for traditional purposes. If a ritual is a series of acts that have always been performed in the same way, it means that you can also adopt rituals in your daily life. As we are about to see, a ritual can be more effective, more confidence-focused and more purposeful.

DO YOU HAVE A DAILY RITUAL?

Some of you probably nodded at this question and thought, "Yes, I do" and visualized the automatic tasks you did this morning as soon as you woke up: snooze your alarm clock, check your phone, brush your teeth, gulp down your breakfast and rush out of the door. Many of us go through a similar scenario every day and it becomes part of who we are. But that's a routine, not a ritual. What's the difference, you ask? By definition, rituals and routines are somewhat similar. Both are a series of actions, tasks or behaviors that you follow regularly. What sets them apart though is the intention and attitude behind the action(s) you take.

With routines, you do them because you have to.

With rituals, you do them because you want to.

A routine exists to give your day structure. We do them without consciously thinking about them. Rituals require thoughtfulness. They are created with meaning and purpose to accomplish a specific goal.

ROUTINES	RITUALS
Minimal engagement	Full engagement
Tedious and meaningless	Symbolic and meaningful
Externally motivated	Internally motivated
Life as a duty	Life as a celebration
Dull awareness	Bright awareness
Disconnected series of events	Tells a story
Focus only on completion of tasks	Focus on the performance of tasks

WHY DO YOU NEED A RITUAL?

Routines are essential to our lives. We need the sense of security, order and consistency that they provide. Thanks to our routines, we don't have to think about small decisions in our lives all the time. We can approach specific tasks on autopilot. Because our routines are predictable, they help us stay organized and in control of our days, and truth be told, we would be lost without them.

Now, imagine how your life could be with more engagement, meaning and motivation. How would you feel? What would you accomplish? You would probably spend less time on things that don't matter and get more done. Research has shown that rituals not only boost our confidence and focus but enhance our overall performance. Rituals put a stronger emphasis on purpose, engagement and enjoyment. In a nut shell, they help us improve our effectiveness.

Routines help you feel safe.
Rituals will make you brave.

If this is not enough to convince you of their value, look no further than high-performance athletes and successful entrepreneurs. They all use rituals to help them get to the top. It's well documented that athletes in particular adopt all types of rituals, albeit some of them rather superstitiously. The six-time NBA basketball champion, Michael Jordan, wore his old college shorts under his Chicago Bulls shorts throughout his career. Rafael Nadal purportedly takes a shower 45 minutes before every tennis match, and Tiger Woods always wore a red shirt on Sundays during golf tournaments since going pro in 1996. These rituals appear to work—all three of them have had wildly successful careers.

Now, you're probably thinking that maybe if you started wearing the yellow shirt your mother gave you for Christmas on Mondays you'd get promoted sooner. Or perhaps if you wore that old varsity sweater before your next interview you'd get the gig. Sorry to disappoint you.

Rituals are transformative but they are personal.

Rituals are not the sole preserve of ultra-performers and superstars. We can all benefit from improving our performance and well-being by adopting rituals that could add tremendous impact to our lives. The best rituals are the ones that stem from your set of values. You won't be able to pick up someone else's rituals just because it has been said that it helped them be happier or more successful. Someone's ritual could be positive, but if you were to try the same thing, it could be more of a burden or a hindrance. Before you know it, it could be taking from your life rather than adding to it. That's why it's best to develop a set of rituals that align with your values and speak to your life's purpose. Ultimately, that's how you will gain more well-being, alignment and focus in your life.

FINDING YOUR RITUAL(S)

If you want to go from the mundane to the extraordinary, consider incorporating small rituals in your day-to-day life. The goal is not to pack your day with so many rituals that you become stressed out. You can even decide to have just one ritual and that's perfectly fine. When and where to practice your ritual doesn't matter as much as the "what" and the "how". You can practice yours in the morning, at mid-day or in the evening, or you can do all three. You could also implement rituals in different aspects of your life. What's important is the personal connection that you have with your ritual. Make sure that it's unique and of your choosing. So, where should you start? Here are some ideas to get you thinking about what yours could be:

IN ACTION: EXPLORE A DAILY RITUAL PRACTICE

Instead of:	Consider this:
Jumping out of bed at the sound of your alarm clock.	**Take time** to soak in the morning atmosphere and enjoy the sounds of nature.
Checking your email as soon as you wake up.	**Brew** your favorite beverage. Take time to sip it and savor the flavor.
Starting the day without any plan.	**Establish** a daily routine for exercising, meditation, prayer and deep breathing.
Entertaining negative thoughts.	**Write out** daily affirmations. You can have affirmations for every area of your life.
Using your phone or tablet in bed.	**Read** a couple of pages of a great book or your favorite blog.
Falling asleep while scrolling through social media.	**Visualize** your goals before bed.

BOLDER STORY

With

BENJAMIN FRANKLIN

Benjamin Franklin, one of America's most famous Founding Fathers, maintained a set of daily rituals throughout his life (see below). What stood out for me is the way his rituals were built around these two questions:

1. Morning: what good should I do today?

2. Evening: what good have I done today?

SCHEME.

	Hours.	
MORNING. The *Question*. What good shall I do this day?	5 6 7	Rise, wash, and address *Powerful Goodness!* Contrive day's business, and take the resolution of the day; prosecute the present study, and breakfast.
	8 9 10 11	Work.
NOON.	12 1	Read, or look over my accounts, and dine.
AFTERNOON.	2 3 4 5	Work.
EVENING. The *Question*. What good have I done to-day?	6 7 8 9	Put things in their places. Supper. Music or diversion, or conversation. Examination of the day.
NIGHT.	10 11 12 1 2 3 4	Sleep.

(From Benjamin Franklin's autobiography)

These simple yet powerful questions are reminders that you can build your rituals around values that are meaningful to you.

139

A BOLDER YOU

In Action

FIND YOUR RITUAL

Finding the right kind of rituals to adopt is not a matter of science but a matter of preference. To develop the best rituals for your life, here are three questions to consider:

1. **What brings you joy?** Do more of that. Take a look at the daily habits that you already have. Which ones bring joy to you? Take these habits and make them more intentional by transforming them into rituals. For example, maybe you have a habit of rushing through a cup of coffee in the morning. You can turn it into a ritual by taking the time to brew the coffee and sitting down to enjoy it.

2. **What causes you pain?** By paying attention to the areas of your life where you are struggling, or where you feel the most tension, you could develop your next rituals. Perhaps it's hard for you to sleep peacefully at night. What ritual could you adopt to ease yourself into better sleep? Once you can identify the areas that cause you the most tension, you can do things to improve them.

3. **What do the people you admire do?** Ask, seek and knock. Find out what the people you look up to do. The goal is not to copy and paste what they are doing, but to open your mind to the things that could help you.

CHAPTER 14

The Rules To Break

—

"Don't let your dreams be limited by what others are

allowing you to achieve."

—ANONYMOUS

I wish I could say that I'm somewhat of a daredevil, a rebel without a cause, the kind of outlaw you see in comic books and Hollywood movies.

But I'm not.

I do break rules though. The type of rules that limit thriving. The ones that I had adopted from well-meaning people in my life. They were the unwritten rules and established norms that kept me stuck in a rut, holding me back from being my authentic self. Yes, those rules. I'm unapologetic about breaking them, and I think you should consider doing so too.

WHY DO WE HAVE RULES?

Rules are guidelines and principles that are established within communities to regulate certain activities. Rules serve a purpose. They govern our behaviors to keep us safe and to prevent chaos. Whether you want to go to school, board a flight or play a sport, there are rules to follow. There are all kinds of rules, and they are everywhere. There's no doubt that rules are essential for law and order in our world. Regulations are intended to protect us, to help create harmony, and in most disciplines, they serve as guiding principles that we probably wouldn't have had otherwise.

Right.

No, I'm not about to go out and trash the streets just because I want to be wild and rebellious. Breaking rules just for the sake of defiance and hurting people is not normal, and I'm certainly not advocating that you do that. What I'm encouraging you to do is to take a closer look at all those unquestioned, common rules that you may have accepted as the gospel truth. I'm talking about those rules that keep you confined to your comfort zone and prevent you from living the extraordinary life you've long desired. Those norms may have benefited others, but you must not forget: someone else's rules will not get you where you want in life.

RULES ARE MEANT TO BE BROKEN

Honestly, where's the growth? Where's the fun? If rules cannot be broken, I don't want to play! Have you ever imagined a world without rules, laws and everything in between? What you pictured looked scary, didn't it? Now, imagine the opposite: a world where there was no way to change the rules. Think about all of the rules that have been put in place that are oppressive, demeaning and dehumanizing. What if no one had challenged them? What if no one dared to think about a different way of doing things?

How many people out there have had their basic rights denied because it was more important to preserve the status quo? How many people are denied opportunities because no one else was bold enough to challenge these so-called rules at the time?

We need to break the rules not just for ourselves but because future generations deserve more—way more!

Breaking the rules is not just about us. When rules are broken, discoveries are made. It allows economic and social change to take place. If civil rights icon Rosa Parks didn't refuse to give up her seat on that bus, if the Wright brothers didn't go through with their plan, and if countless others simply obeyed the rules to the letter, we wouldn't be where we are today. Sometimes the rules we have to break are societal, an injustice that we can no longer tolerate. But sometimes the rules we need to break are the ones that we have accepted and made our own. It's these rules that hold us back from living our best lives.

WHAT'S HOLDING YOU BACK?

Scratch that.

The real question is: whose rules are you living by? Living by other people's rules stops us from getting what we want in life. Often, we don't even realize that we've adopted rules that act as barriers by preventing us from realizing our dreams. For example, the advert for a job you want to apply for states that you need five years of relevant experience but you only have two. You meet all the other criteria but you convince yourself not to apply because you know what the "rules" are.

Are you being crippled by rules? Do any of these scenarios sound familiar?

- You've convinced yourself that you can't change careers because you didn't study towards a particular field.

- You believe you need to work in your company for a certain number of years before asking for a promotion.

- You want to take a sabbatical but you think you can't take a break from the workplace because, well, it would be hard for you to get another job when you're ready to return.

- You're afraid of ruffling feathers by taking the road less traveled.

If you identify with this, you're not alone. All kinds of commandments for life are conveyed to us from when we're young. We're instructed to follow certain conventions as time-tested statutes to live by. As children, even when we dare to ask why we must do things in a certain way we're told "that's just the way it is." As adults, many of us continue on this path of adopting advice, beliefs and principles as roadmaps for our lives. We repeat our childhood ways and ask no questions because "that's just the way it is."

Just because it worked before for other people doesn't mean it will work for you. And because it works doesn't mean that there's not a better way you can do it. The fact of the matter is that the "right path" you've been advertised is not wrong, but it's also not necessarily right. It all depends on who you are, the values you hold dear and what you want out of life. We've copied and pasted rules in our lives that come from our friends' and family's lives. But if you want to get things you've never had, go places you've never been and achieve things that you've always wanted, then you need to question the rules being presented to you continually. Ask those questions internally and externally, and be honest with yourself. If those so-called rules are holding you back from being the best version of yourself, dare to break them.

We follow these rules blindly even though all they do is stifle our growth. We stop ourselves from pursuing new careers, we fail to explore fantastic adventures and we don't take the chance to live in a new country because we're told that we can't do it. The simple fact that you're reading this book meant that I broke a so-called rule that says you have to have a big six-figure deal with an equally big publishing house before you can get your story told. Conventional life and career wisdom will advise you to take the sure bet. There is merit in that, of course. Play it safe and there are no regrets to have. But do keep in mind that every successful enterprise and every big breakthrough has come about as a result of someone breaking a couple of rules along the way.

A breakthrough is just that: you have to break through the rules, the assumptions, the fears, the risks to get where you want to be.

There's more progress to be made, and you will only make it by stepping beyond what's already been done to chart a new course for yourself. But first some rules.

THE RULES OF RULE BREAKING

There are rules for everything, remember?

Breaking the rules is risky—there are things to consider before breaking out. Breaking the rules is a conscious decision and must be intentional. You must intentionally decide to go for what you want. You have to be a rebel but only with a cause (e.g. your quest to live your best life) and there are things you must take into account. Being a rule-breaker means that regardless of whether you succeed or fail you must make your own decisions. And you must be prepared to handle the outcomes of those decisions. In the words of Rwandan president Paul Kagame, "We don't follow rules. We follow choices. There is no rule book for us. If things work for us, we celebrate. If they don't, we don't blame anybody. We look back and ask where did we go wrong?"

What choices do you want to follow?

If breaking the rules is about making choices, it's also up to you to mitigate the risks. Dr. E.J. Leverett, a pioneer in risk management, came up with these three rules that I think are useful when considering breaking the rules. Here they are:

1. Don't risk a lot for a little.

2. Don't risk more than you can afford to lose.

3. Consider the odds and the consequences.

BE A SUCCESSFUL RULE BREAKER

As the Dalai Lama said, "Know the rules well, so you can break them effectively." I will be the first to admit that I want you to break the rules that are holding you back, but I want you to do it while putting all the chances to succeed on your side. For that, consider ...

IN ACTION: BREAKING RULES EFFECTIVELY	
Instead of:	**Consider this:**
Following someone's rule-breaking playbook.	**Break rules in your own lane and in your own way** by staying true to yourself and the values you hold dear.
Blindly breaking rules and waiting to see what happens.	**Think about** the consequences and the risks involved.
Playing it safe and being scared of failure.	**Get comfortable** with failure.

BOLDER STORY

With

MADAM C.J. WALKER

Before Avon, Mary Kay and Fenty Beauty, there was Madam C.J. Walker Beauty Culture—a hair and beauty line for black women.

Born Sarah Breedlove, Madam C.J. Walker was the founder of her eponymous brand and became America's first female self-made millionaire as recorded in the Guinness Book of World Records. Madam C.J. Walker was an unlikely candidate for such incredible success. Born to enslaved parents, she was orphaned at 7, got married at 14, became a mother when she was 17 and was widowed by 20. But her life challenges and tragedies also fueled her incredible journey towards entrepreneurship. Her struggle with hair loss inspired her to create hair and skincare products that would complement African-American women's beauty, not detract from it.

The Madam C.J. Walker brand was born at the turn of the 20th century. An innovator and skilled marketer, Madam C.J. initially sold her products door to door before building one of Indianapolis' most significant factories. Despite her circumstances and lack of resources, Madam C.J. Walker took the risk of becoming self-employed and invented her products, selling them her way by leveraging door-to-door sales marketing. And as she used to say, "I got my start by giving myself a start."

Give yourself the start you need!

A BOLDER YOU

In Action

RE-WRITING THE RULES

What kind of starts should you be giving yourself?

When all's said and done, it's still your life. And if you're not thriving, then it's probably time to re-write the rules that are holding you back.

Ready to shake things up? Follow these three steps to break free:

1. **Awareness:** pay attention to how you run through your day, the things you do and say and how you behave. Do you always greet people the same way? Do you reply to emails in a specific manner? Do you only speak up in meetings when spoken to? Take note of the rules you are following.

2. **Access:** write down what you notice. You can use the format below or just write it wherever you like. Are those rules holding you back or propelling you forward? How are they supporting your goals?

3. **Adjust:** the goal is to thrive, and if those rules aren't benefitting you then it's time for them to go. For example, if one of your rules is never to greet strangers but your goal in life is to make more friends, how will that happen?

CHAPTER 15

Rising Strong

—

"You show me anybody that's great in anything

they do, I'll show you somebody that's persevered,

demonstrated that mental toughness to overcome some

obstacles and adversity."

—SEAN MCVAY

Have you ever wondered how some people can persevere through hardships while others can't? How is it possible that two people can go through the same life experiences yet their perspectives and coping mechanisms are so different? What then is the difference between these people? Are they genetically superior? Do they have a unique talent? Did they crack the code to an ancient secret?

Far from it. The answer is mental toughness.

THE MENTALLY STRONG

When someone is deemed mentally strong, it's usually a reference to that person's inner strength, ability to cope with the ups and downs of life and the way they bounce back from adversity. There are countless stories of people who've managed to overcome significant tragedies and defy great odds. We hear about these stories in the press, in movies and through documentaries and books. But people like that are not works of fiction. They are ordinary people just like you and me who end up leading extraordinary lives in part because of their mental strength. They are all around us. You know the one who always finds the positive and the funny side in difficult situations. We all know the one who gets knocked down but never seems to stay down. Everybody has met someone who doesn't feel sorry for themselves when they have every reason to do so. I think we all know at least one person in our lives who would qualify as mentally strong.

My friend Nina is one of those people.

When Ladydi, Nina's sister, passed on, we were all shattered. Ladydi was within our sisterhood, the glue that kept us together. A bubbly, kind-hearted soul with so many gifts to share with the world. "Gone too soon" was an understatement. While most of us were still reeling from the loss, Nina powered on through the pain. She chose to focus on Ladydi's well-lived albeit short life, finding lessons in an inexplicable event, and trying to find the good in a tragic situation. I realized then that if she was still standing and moving forward, it was at least partly due to her mental strength. Her attitude and approach to life had inspired me to up my mental strength.

What about you?

ARE YOU MENTALLY STRONG?

We live in a less-than-perfect world, and sooner or later certain things will go wrong. Life is unpredictable. We will all be tested by unexpected challenges—the loss of a loved one, a job that's made redundant, the end of a relationship and so on.

How do you react when faced with challenges?

- You're a pessimist and see difficulties as long-lasting.

- You get overwhelmed with feelings of anger, sadness and discouragement when a bad situation occurs.

- You think you are cursed with bad luck and life is against you every time an unfortunate situation arises.

- You can't see how things will work out in your favor.

Or do you have the confidence and the strength of character to rise to the challenge? To see setbacks as opportunities for growth. Although it's normal to feel a host of emotions when confronted with challenges and life-altering events, the ability to overcome them plays a huge part in our success or failure in life.

BENEFITS OF BEING MENTALLY STRONG

Being mentally strong is the key to thriving and achieving long-term success. When you're mentally strong, everything improves: your thoughts, your energy and your emotions.

Cultivating mental strength will help you:

✓ **Develop more confidence:** everyone experiences self-doubt at some point in time, but when you are mentally strong you can reframe your negative self-talk into self-empowerment. You can hold on to the confidence necessary to accomplish your goals, and you are more prepared when confronted with hardships.

✓ **Strengthen your focus:** being mentally strong will help you clarify what you want, why you want it and help you define how to get it. You'll no longer be dependent on others to light the path for you, and you'd have more focus to aim higher and go deeper.

✓ **Gain resilience:** being mentally strong will give you wings to face your fears. You'll have the courage to step out of your comfort zone and conquer life like you haven't done before. You will also be able to make rational decisions and not be led by your emotions.

MENTAL STRENGTH IS NOT ...

When I speak of being mentally strong, it doesn't mean that you don't have emotions and never show them. It's okay to feel sad, angry or disappointed. What it means is that you don't let your emotions overwhelm you. You have the confidence to keep going, to keep believing that the tough times may come but won't last. Being mentally strong doesn't mean that you hide behind toughness, acting as though nothing leaves you shaken. It's not about masking the pain, the suffering and the emotions you are dealing with. Nina certainly did not do that. I saw her cry. I saw her sad. But I also saw her trying to take a step forward by holding on to the reminder that even dark seasons don't stop the sun from shining.

BECOMING MENTALLY STRONG

So, are we born mentally tough or do we have to nurture it? Numerous studies have been done on the subject, and while the outcome remains in flux, what's certain is that we can learn to be mentally strong. You must cultivate this strength because if you don't, it will eventually cost you. Mental strength is something you have to find within. Similar to physical strength, it's like a muscle and doesn't grow by accident. It has to be developed. "Faking it till you make it" won't work here. Building mental strength requires dedication, effort and consistency. Building and strengthening your mental muscle is a lifelong process.

IN ACTION: BUILDING MENTAL TOUGHNESS	
Instead of:	**Consider this:**
Losing faith and trust in your ability to move forward.	**Visualize** the outcomes you want.
Losing faith and trust in your ability to move forward.	**Improving your self-talk**—refer to the *Braver Tip* in chapter 4 to refresh your memory.
Dwelling on negative thoughts and only seeing negative possibilities.	**Get into the daily practice** of celebrating daily wins by writing down your top three WWWs (What is Working Well) at the end of day.

BOLDER STORY

With

BETHANY HAMILTON

What do you do when your dream, purpose and passion is almost snatched from you? What do you do when life throws a wrench in your plans? Do you fight back or do you let it define you?

Bethany Hamilton didn't let it define her.

In 2003 when Bethany was just 13 years old, a 14-foot tiger shark severed her left arm while she was out surfing the ocean. If that wasn't enough of a devastating blow, the fact that she lost her arm below the shoulder made it difficult for her to wear a prosthetic arm so she had to re-learn how to surf using just one arm.

Anyone going through a tragedy like this would have been devastated and probably given up on their dream. But instead of letting this unfortunate incident define her, she rose to the challenge. Heartbroken but undeterred, she taught herself how to surf again and returned to the sport she loved so much just 26 days after her attack. By 2007, she realized her lifelong ambition of becoming a professional surfer.

In the years since her shark attack, Bethany has been unstoppable. She's gone on to win several competitions around the world, overcoming incredible odds to achieve greatness. Her unbelievably positive attitude and deep faith have demonstrated that even though life is unpredictable, and we will all face our share of ups and downs, it's possible to keep going and thriving.

A BOLDER YOU

In Action

NEGATIVE VISUALIZATION

Life happens, and while we can't control what is thrown at us, we can control our reaction instead of being caught off guard. But how?

By using what is called *negative visualization*. The concept dates back to the great stoic philosophers who called it *premeditatio malorum* or premeditation of evils. According to Nassim Taleb, a stoic is "someone who transforms fear into prudence, pain into transformation, mistakes into initiation, and desire into undertaking." So, this exercise inspired by the Stoics is about being ready for disruption, and imagining worst-case scenarios about events in your life. By doing this, you'll be better equipped to respond to them rather than be overwhelmed by them.

How do you practice it?

1. Take any situation that you're dealing with in your life. Maybe you are starting to look for a job, about to buy a house or planning to move to a new city.

2. Ask yourself what could go wrong. Think about all the bad things that could happen.

3. Imagine that these situations are happening right now, how would you react?

4. Now think about how you could prepare for those things. What could you do now to minimize the impact of these scenarios?

CHAPTER 16

Breaking Habits, Making Habits

—

"People do not decide their futures; they decide their

habits and their habits decide their futures."

—F. MATTHIAS ALEXANDER

I think, you lack motivation," Zoya said mockingly, while fidgeting on her phone for the umpteenth time.

"What do you mean, and why would you say such a thing?" I replied, shocked by such a daring declaration.

Undeterred, Zoya stood up from her desk and walked to pick up the cup of coffee on my desk.

"What's this?" she asked.

I tried to change the subject and said, "I like your new hairdo," with a sheepish smile.

"Whatever," she responded while holding my cup of coffee. "Isn't this THE coffee you decided to give up three months ago? You started so well, at least during the first few weeks. Now look at you! I guess old habits die hard, huh?" she smirked while walking away.

Did she just give me a lecture about habits? I was puzzled. That was my line. Anyone who knows me knows that I always call out and nag people about their limiting behaviors. And here she calls me out.

It hurt.

The caffeine was hurting too. The strawberry-sized pimples had taken over my face. My sluggish and dull skin was a good enough reminder of my over-reliance on coffee to power me through the day. Did I want to kick the coffee habit? Yes. Was I motivated to develop a healthier habit? Of course, yes—and that's why I was so shocked by Zoya's less-than-kind suggestion that I wasn't doing all I could to change my ways.

I really did want to stop drinking coffee. I watched motivational videos on the internet. I subscribed to endless encouragement-loaded podcasts. I woke up to motivational posters. I had enough motivational frequencies in me to launch a radio show! That's how motivated I was to break my habit.

But I guess my motivation wasn't enough.

We all start so well by making resolutions, writing down goals, coming up with plans and hoping things will be different this time around. We're always super excited at the beginning of the journey. We talk a good game, write out our to-do lists and let the whole world know that our best self is coming out. But soon enough we end up just like politicians—all talk and no action!

THE MOTIVATION MYTH

Motivation can be an internal and external driving force that pushes you to act. In my case the motivation was internal. I simply wanted to improve my health and I was on a quest to overcome the coffee monster. Coffee is good but wasn't right for me. I had enough symptoms to prove that I needed to edit that habit out of my life. I was motivated but I wasn't getting closer to kicking this bad habit to the curb. Where was I going wrong? As personal development guru Jim Rohn remarked, "Motivation alone is not enough. If you have an idiot, and you motivate him, now you have a motivated idiot."

Ouch.

As helpful as motivation is, the bottom line is that you can't trust it. There are days when we're pumped up to go after our goals, tackle our to-do lists and create the best version of ourselves. We feel like we could take on anything that comes our way. Then there are those days when even seeing an alien outside your window wouldn't spur any movement. We just don't feel like doing anything. Relying on motivation alone to get stuff done will do that to you. The inspiration quickly evaporates and you wave goodbye to all of your well-meaning plans for change. It gets worse because we sit and wait for the feeling to come back, and when it doesn't, we feel like a failure because now we haven't accomplished what we set out to do.

Motivation's temporary nature makes it an unreliable ally to count on when aiming to make long-lasting changes in our lives. Motivation comes and goes. So, if we can't rely on our motivation to fuel us to long-term change, what should we do?

Build good habits.

BUILDING GOOD HABITS

Former Olympic athlete Jim Ryun said, "While motivation can get you started, habit is what will keep you going." Habits are behaviors that you do without even thinking about them. Research indicates that about 40% of our actions are habits that are automated. You think you're making a decision, but in most cases you aren't. Whether we like it or not, our habits control our lives. And they are what often stands between where we are now and the change we want to see.

Most of us want to exercise more, eat better and spend less money. We get psyched up and dive straight in. Then we're surprised when the habit doesn't stick. We give up and feel useless. So, we pick another pattern that we want to change. When that doesn't work out we become discouraged and wave the white flag of surrender. The truth is that we simply don't understand how our habits are formed. We just want to snap our fingers and erase the bad ones. But understanding how they are developed is the first step towards building new and sustainable habits.

HOW ARE HABITS FORMED?

Every habit is a three-part process. A smart guy named Charles Duhigg came up with the habit loop concept. Essentially, the habit loop has these three parts: the cue, the routine and the reward. These are essential to not only understand how habits are formed but also to know how we can change to adopt better ones:

- **The cue** is what triggers your habit or behavior. In my case, it's the time of the day. I wake up at 6 a.m. and know that it's time for my morning coffee.

- **The routine** is the actual habit. It's tuning in to your favorite radio station straight after waking up, or brushing your teeth as soon as you've jumped out of bed.

- **The reward** is the last part of the process. This is the feeling you get once you've executed the habit. It serves to strengthen the relationship between the trigger and your behavior.

Tying all of this back to my coffee problem:

- My cue: arriving at work at 8 a.m. every day.

- My behavior: I make a cup of coffee.

- My reward: the feeling of caffeine running through my body, waking me up and giving me energy.

I know, I know. You're thinking this sounds so serious and hard. It's not. As you'll see in our *In Action* exercise of the day, it's easier than you think to build new, better habits. But how long does it take to form new habits? Well, that depends on who you ask.

THE PROCESS OF FORMING NEW HABITS

Many of us want sudden behavioral change. We like overnight success stories, and we want our process of changing our habits to mirror those. That's why we tend to be attracted to things that promise to be fast, painless and free. Get rich quick schemes, seven days to an MBA, 48 hours to eliminate back pain—all types of offers that claim to get us to our goals faster. All that you're likely to get from these are guaranteed failures.

Some people claim that forming a new habit takes 21 days, others say it takes 30 days. A study at the University of London reported that, on average, it takes about 66 days before a new habit can be formed, and that still depends on the person. Regardless of which one you believe, your focus should not be on speed but on consistency. Besides, think about it: how long did it take you to develop that bad habit in the first place? Two years? Ten years? You probably don't remember anymore. So don't worry about the amount of time that it will take you. It's more important to be consistent. After all, you're in this for the long haul, not instant, but ultimately fleeting, success.

Be bold enough in embracing the small beginning and the tiny steps you take. They will eventually add up and create the significant change you seek.

You can still build good habits and create positive changes by starting out small. Change doesn't have to be dramatic as we're often told and sold. Small steps lead to habits that lead to long-lasting changes. Consider:

IN ACTION: BUILDING NEW HABITS	
Instead of:	**Consider this:**
Wanting to start big.	**Start small.** We explore how to do this in our *In Action* exercise of the day.
Wanting to change many habits at once.	**Be specific** and focus on one habit at a time.
Relying on your old ways of doing things.	**Try changing** your environment and removing barriers so it can be conducive to the changes you seek.

BOLDER TIP

By

DR. BJ FOGG

Dr. BJ Fogg has pioneered the Fogg Method: a three-step plan for creating new habits. At the heart of the technique is the concept of tiny habits. Tiny habits are personal behaviors that you practice at least once a day for 30 minutes or less and requires little effort. Dr. Fogg believes that the key to changing a behavior is by making the habit ridiculously tiny and gaining success from the little-by-little progress one makes.

Follow these five steps to build your own tiny habits:

1. **Choose a small behavioral change you want to make**

   Do one push up a day for example.

2. **Anchor it to one of your existing habits**

   Say you meditate every day. Do the push up straight after your meditation session.

3. **Reward yourself after accomplishing your new behavior**

   Smile, dance, say "yay" or do what you do to celebrate.

4. **Increase the level of difficulty over time**

   Do one push up a day for the first week. Then increase it to two the following week and so on.

5. **Stay consistent**

   After a few weeks this tiny habit will be fully automatic, and you should be able to do it without thinking.

FORMING A NEW HABIT

What is one habit that you already have that can be an anchor? (Do that habit in step1)

_____
_____
_____
_____
_____
_____
_____
_____

What is the habit you want to build? (Step2)

_____
_____
_____
_____
_____
_____
_____

How would you celebrate this new habit? (Step 3)

_____
_____
_____
_____
_____
_____
_____
_____

In summary, to form a new habit, the formula is:

After I	I will	& celebrate by

Inspired by BJ Fogg's method

CHAPTER 17

Getting Things Done

—

"Procrastination is the grave in which

opportunity is buried."

—ALYCE CORNYN-SELBY

Tomorrow is another day.

Ever heard that saying? I bet you've even used it at some point in your life. How many times have you put something off that could be done now because, well, tomorrow is another day?

If "tomorrow is another day" could talk, I wonder what tales it would tell. It would probably tell us stories about the countless ideas that never materialized, the books that were never published and the untapped potential that was left dormant all because people like you and I believed the whispers sung by "tomorrow is another day."

Putting things off to a later date starts out small, then becomes a habit and before you know it, it becomes full-on procrastination. Whenever you procrastinate, you don't just miss doing what you should get done, you miss out on opportunities and the world moves on without you.

A VILLAIN CALLED PROCRASTINATION

The most common definition of procrastination is "the voluntary delay of an intended act despite the knowledge that this delay may harm us." Procrastination is tempting, and its voice can be so darn comforting. Procrastination will hit all the right notes when giving you endless reasons why you should avoid doing something. It will tell you that you're working too hard, that you deserve those extra ten minutes scrolling through social media and that you should go out shopping. It will convince you that you can always come back later to finish that important project because you know, well, everything you're working so hard on will still be there when you come back tomorrow.

But the "still be there" part is where it goes wrong. It means the same old thing will keep happening. It means nothing will change, and you'll fail to move forward. "Later" and "still be there" are two sides of the same coin and not friends to cozy up to. They make you lazy and keep you stuck. Then you will only have yourself to blame.

DO YOU PROCRASTINATE?

"Everyone procrastinates, but not everyone is a procrastinator."

—JOSEPH FERRARI

So, can you procrastinate but not be a procrastinator? Yes, sort of.

We all procrastinate to a certain level. Most of us have been guilty at least once of waiting till the last minute to write an email, finish off a project or return a call. Procrastinating is in itself human, but procrastination can slowly turn into a self-defeating and damaging habit. Many people are regarded as casual procrastinators because they avoid doing some tasks in very specific situations. But the kind of procrastination I'm referring to is habitual procrastination. Habitual procrastinators, also called chronic procrastinators, find it challenging to complete tasks in general. A chronic procrastinator will struggle to finish work-related, personal, financial or social tasks in their life.

Do any of these statements apply to you?

- You frequently say that you'll do something tomorrow, and make lots of excuses for why you're not doing it.

- You often waste time on other things rather than focusing on your deadlines.

- You put things off until you're very close to or past the deadline.

- You use distraction to avoid thinking about the essential areas of your life.

- You wait for "inspiration" before starting on the tasks at hand.

- You start new projects before finishing off old ones.

If you identify with any of these, you could very well be a chronic procrastinator. But don't despair, you're not alone. Research suggests that 1 in 5 people could be considered a chronic procrastinator. Before you pat yourself on the back just because there are many others out there like you, remember this: procrastination is the enemy of your success. Nothing worth accomplishing in your life will happen if you don't reign in your procrastination. Knowing that you are a chronic procrastinator is just one side of the equation. If you want to get ahead, you need to understand why you do it and how to eliminate it from your life.

WHY DO WE PROCRASTINATE?

You can't fix what you don't know. Understanding the root causes of procrastination is as powerful and as necessary as fighting it. So, why do we procrastinate? It's not necessarily what you think. You know the saying, "It's not you, it's me?" Well, procrastination is all about that happening within.

Procrastination is about emotions:

The common misconception about procrastination is that it's all about laziness. To a certain degree, laziness plays a part. We're lazy enough to just focus on what we need to focus on, but that doesn't mean that we're idle. Even when we're procrastinating, we're doing something. Think about it—we find time to bake, scroll through social media, browse the net or busy ourselves with everything but the urgent and necessary stuff! So it's not that we lack the time or run out of it to do what should be done. As Professor Dr. Tim Pychyl discovered in his research, our procrastination is not a time management problem but an emotion regulation problem. It's basically a coping mechanism. For what? Well, we procrastinate because of the discomfort we feel about the task. The task could be making us feel insecure or incompetent.

In his research Dr. Pychyl identified seven triggers that make it easy to procrastinate. We're more likely to procrastinate when the things we have to do in our lives are:

- Boring
- Frustrating
- Difficult
- Ambiguous
- Unstructured
- Not intrinsically rewarding
- Lacking in personal meaning

Let's say, for example, you have to drive to meet an acquaintance in a city far from you. Suppose you deem that meeting this person will be boring and not intrinsically rewarding. In that case, you're more likely to put it off indefinitely. We procrastinate to feel better because we're afraid of dealing with the emotions being brought to the fore because of the task.

Procrastination is about limiting beliefs:

Limiting or false beliefs that we accept about ourselves hold us back. Because of low self-esteem, we're afraid of attempting specific tasks. We think we'll fail or assume we're simply just not good enough. So we don't even try. An example of a false belief is "I work better under pressure." I know that one all too well. Once we've convinced ourselves of that, we'll wait until the last minute to get the work done. Invariably, the quality of the work is compromised.

Procrastination is a fight:

Procrastination is a fight between our present self and our future self. Our present self wants instant gratification. We want to indulge in things now and neglect future concerns. Recent research from academic Hal Hershfield suggests that when we're disconnected from our future selves in that manner, it becomes easier to put things off and develop into chronic procrastinators. The result? We'll struggle to make long-term plans, we'll make incorrect decisions and fail to realize our goals.

OVERCOMING PROCRASTINATION

We talked about the root causes of procrastination and addressed some of the reasons behind it. But now, how do we solve it? Procrastination is problematic and overcoming it requires managing your emotions effectively. As I mentioned earlier, it's not a time management issue per se, it's an emotional issue. Learning how to manage your emotions and fighting the false beliefs behind your habitual procrastination are the right steps toward kicking the habit. While there are many strategies you can adopt to overcome procrastination, here are a few recommendations to consider:

IN ACTION: KICKING PROCRASTINATION TO THE CURB	
Instead of:	**Consider this:**
Being overwhelmed by big items on your to-do list.	**Break down** your list of tasks into small chunks so you can feel empowered to keep going. We'll explore this further in our *In Action* exercise of the day.
Berating yourself for procrastinating in the past.	**Forgive yourself** knowing that you will do better in future.
Ignoring how you feel about your tasks and burying your head in the sand.	**Choose a mindfulness practice** like journaling, meditation or a breathing practice to get in touch with yourself.
Forcing yourself to accomplish everything on your list.	**Make accomplishing your tasks fun** by giving yourself a reward for getting through each one on your list.

BOLDER TIP

By

MEL ROBBINS

Acclaimed author, TV host and motivational speaker Mel Robbins has a simple yet effective approach to overcoming procrastination: the 5 Second Rule. Robbins' 5 Second Rule is based on the premise that there's a five second window between the moment you decide to do something and your mind sabotaging it all together.

The 5 Second Rule works like this:

1. **Feel:** the moment you desire to act on a goal, you must do it immediately or within five seconds. Otherwise your brain will start leaning towards procrastination.

2. **Count backward:** 5-4-3-2-1.

3. **Move:** as soon as you reach "1" you move and do the task you want to do.

Why does it work? The 5 Second Rule is a way of tricking your brain and beating it at its own game by distracting it from the various ways it could be sabotaging you. So next time you're tempted to hit the "snooze" button or feel like abandoning your daily run, just do the 5-4-3-2-1 count. Besides Robbins' groundbreaking tip, I'm recommending an approach on the next page to reviewing your procrastination and the steps you need to take to combat it.

GETTING THINGS DONE

The most important tasks I did not accomplish:

Here is the reason for my procrastination:
(I find the tasks to be...)

- Boring   _____
- Unpleasant   _____
- Difficult   _____
- Overwhelming   _____
- Other   _____

To get back on track, I will break down the task into smaller parts
(Go through this for each task)

- First, I will do   _____
- Second, I will do   _____
- Third, I will do   _____
- Fourth, I will do   _____
- Fifth, I will do   _____

I will complete this task by:

I will reward myself by:

CHAPTER 18

Destination Goal

———

"People with goals succeed because they

know where they're going."

—EARTH NIGHTINGALE

One of my favorite childhood memories was when my friends and I were at school, under the shades of trees, sharing and debating over the dreams we held. Our aspirations ranged from getting the most prominent house or getting a Ph.D., to more grandiose ones that touched on the well-being of our societies: reforms and changes we wanted to see and bring to our respective communities, the schools we wanted to build, the businesses we wanted to start and the access we dreamed of giving to succeeding generations. We were children, yes, but we already had the highest visions for the future. From our vantage point, nothing could stop us, and everything would be in our favor when the time came. Eventually, the time did come, and most never took advantage of it. As adults, these dreams somehow have shifted, bent, and some forgotten altogether. One thing that remains is that out of the countless hopes we shared under the blistering midday sun, many have yet to come to life. But in our group, one person stood out: my friend Lia who accomplished almost every ambition she ever told us about.

Becoming a well-established international lawyer? Check. Taking over the real estate market and growing her portfolio of companies? Check. Going back to her home country to impact young people and be of service to her community? Check. I could go on and on. But what was the difference between Lia and the rest of us? While our childhood conversations about the future remained just talk for most of us, Lia aspired to turn them into reality. Beyond her ironclad discipline and laser focus, she succeeded because she could translate her bold ideas into goals—making them achievable.

DREAMS VS. GOALS

We all love to dream, and who can blame us? We're accustomed to hearing about the need to strive for bigger and better things, and are encouraged to keep these dreams alive even when everything around us is conspiring to make us give up. But what's in a dream? A dream is defined as an "ambition; one that is extremely pleasant, beautiful, or fine." Dreams give us hope, embolden us, and drive us to go after endeavors that are bigger than what our current circumstances show us. But if having aspirations and ambitions were all that it took, why are so many people unaccomplished? Why do so many of our dreams simply gather dust? Because, contrary to popular belief, it's not enough to merely dream.

The most accomplished people in the world were undoubtedly dreamers. There wouldn't be any Disneyland, Microsoft, Amazon, Spanx, and more without individuals who first had clear visions in their minds. But do you know what else they did? They also got to work. Alas, the doing part. That's the step most of us dread. Unfortunately, there's no genie in a bottle to magically make your wishes come true. To go from dreamland to doing-it land, you'll need to turn your dreams into goals. Many of us tend to confuse dreams with goals. They are used interchangeably so often in conversations, but they are not the same. The Cambridge dictionary defines a goal as "an aim, a purpose." While dreams are an inspiration for the future, goals are more realistic. You can be dreaming all day long but goals require action. They require deadlines and deliverables. Goals are the fuel that helps us march towards success. They give us a sense of meaning while helping us improve our decision-making skills and strengthen our commitment.

WINNING WITH GOALS

The most effective way to see your visions materialize is to set specific goals to serve as a compass toward fulfillment. Every time you set goals, you are essentially declaring your commitment to making your dream a reality. Only a few, rational people set goals, and when the rest don't succeed, they blame just about anything to justify their lack of doing. While there are elements outside our control, we can still set ourselves on a path for progress and success by working according to our agenda.

Goals bridge the gap between hopes and reality. And as Denzel Washington said, "Dreams without goals remain dreams and ultimately fuel disappointment." Wishful thinking can be comforting, but it won't make you successful. You can expect all you want, but unless you take action, nothing is going to change. Do you identify with any of the following statements?

- You tend to think in terms of "someday".
- You don't like to make plans or don't take appropriate action.
- You romanticize life and hope a lot but don't back it up with action.
- You struggle with follow-through and easily get discouraged.
- You say "yes" to new ideas quickly but don't get started on any.
- You're easily paralyzed when it's time to make decisions.

Being clear about your plans and implementing practical goal-setting strategies will be the beginning of your victory. Ever driven a car without an engine? Me neither. Our dreams are like cars. If we have no engine to make them move, we end up stuck, angry at ourselves and the world, and simply watch as life passes us by.

GOAL SETTING

As we have established, keeping your dreams in your head won't help them get done. In order to be an achiever, you'll need to:

Begin with the end in mind

This means that you start with your ultimate dream, and then you work backward to develop your goals and plan. By doing so, you can mentally prepare yourself and locate the specific goals you need to reach your destination.

Focus

You'll need direction to make your goals happen. It's easy to be tempted to make a long list of things to do and think you can multitask your way to them. Doing this will only confuse you, and in the end, you'll accomplish little. Focus is strength. Be careful with the plans you make and work on them one at a time rather than overwhelming yourself with plenty.

Make your goals SMART

Not all goals are created equal. In your quest to reach your dreams, you need to set SMART goals. This means that they must be:

- **S**pecific: goals should be clear and concise. A broad and vague one will only leave you frustrated.

- **M**easurable: you need to be able to measure the success of your goals. Being able to do so will help monitor your progress.

- **A**chievable: your goals need to be challenging but doable. Don't go for outrageous ones just for the sake of it.

- **R**elevant: every goal must align with your general purpose and should be based on your current reality, otherwise they'll be meaningless.

- **T**ime-bound: your goals should have a deadline. Know exactly when each goal should be achieved.

Here's an example of a typical goal versus a SMART goal:

"I will exercise every week" compared to "By the end of December, I'll be exercising for 45 minutes each day, three times a week."

Write them down

If you keep everything in your head, you are bound to forget. By writing down your goals, you're more likely to work on them and, in turn, achieve them.

Review your progress

Having tangible milestones for your goals will help you visualize your progress and determine whether or not you need to make adjustments.

Consider the following ideas as well:

IN ACTION: GOAL SETTING

Instead of:	Consider this:
Letting others, the Internet and social media decide for you.	**Decide what you want to do and envision the end game.** What would you like to accomplish? What would success look like for you?
Trying to do too many things at the same time.	**Focus on one goal at a time,** breaking them down into small chunks.
Spending your time only with "dreamers".	**Enlarge your support network** to include "doers", people who are actually accomplishing things instead of just talking about them.
Becoming discouraged when things take time to materialize.	**From the start, assume that things will take longer** and will cost you more so that you don't give up easily when faced with challenges.

BOLDER TIP

With

DAVID ALLEN

Is there a formula for setting goals? How does one get to do it the right way? How do we stick to our goals?

Here are some goal-setting tips from a renowned authority on productivity that could help you out. David Allen is the mastermind behind the Getting Things Done (GTD) productivity system.

Allen recommends doing the following for setting achievable goals:

- **Set short-term process goals:** long-term goals are important but they can be daunting. Instead, focus on setting what he calls "short-term process goals" that are directly linked with the activity and what you'll need to do to make the goal happen. This will help you stay motivated and maintain momentum. Let's say, for example, your goal is to read one book every month. Your process goal could be to read at least 10 pages per day. It's clear and well defined.

- **Build new habits:** your goals won't happen if you don't get rid of bad habits and adopt new ones. It's hard to move forward if you're being held back by old and negative ways of doing things.

- **Get your goals out of your head:** don't use your mind as a repository for your ideas. Use a system, online or offline, to capture your goals.

- **Weekly review:** it's important to step back and review what you have accomplished and to monitor your progress.

A BOLDER YOU

In Action

BACKWARD GOAL-SETTING

We've discussed at length the importance of having goals. We know they make the difference between being focused and being adrift in life. Now it's time to work on our goal-setting capabilities! While there are various techniques one may adopt, there's one in particular which I would like to propose: backward goal-setting.

How to do it?

- Start with the end-goal in mind: what is the ultimate goal that you want to achieve? (Remember to formulate a SMART goal)

- Break your goal into smaller and easier steps: what do you have to do exactly, and how much time do you allocate for it?

- Work back again: take each of the small goals and break them down further to discover what you need to accomplish before milestones are reached.

- Create an action list: from the steps above, you should now have a series of clear actions you need to take to get closer to materializing your plans for the future.

So, for today's exercise, we're going to use the backward setting plan to set a goal you've always wanted to accomplish.

- First, write down your annual SMART goal.

- Now break down the goal into smaller-sized goals and work backwards. Keep working backward until you reach more achievable plans.

- Lastly, summarize the list of immediate actions you need to take and start moving ahead.

CHAPTER 19

Finish What You Start

—

"The only ceiling to your success is your self-discipline. You can go as far as you want to go in life once you bring yourself under control."

—BILLY ALSBROOKS

C an you finish what you've started?

From my seat, I could hear the irritation and the frustration in Lindiwe's voice as she asked Lex, our colleague, that question. I lowered my head and kept typing away, hoping to not be dragged into a conversation that had become quite repetitive. Anyone who has ever worked in a team knows the joy and pain that comes with it. Being an ensemble to innovate and deliver on a goal can be inspiring, to say the least. But, more often than not, the process of getting to the finish line together can be messy and frustrating. As for Lindiwe, this office teamwork situation was turning into the greatest horror show of all time. The team she had put together to deliver on one of the company's flagship projects was falling apart. Lindiwe, plagued by a lack of communication, sinking morale, stressful delays and a colleague not pulling his weight, was at her wits' end. I felt for Lindiwe. By nature, she lived by efficiency, action and commitment, which meant she had no time for slackers and excuse-givers. Anyone who wanted to be part of her team on any given project knew that. Well, everyone except Lex.

Saying that Lex was the opposite of Lindiwe would have been an understatement—Lex was unreliable, uncooperative and a freeloader at best. He was far from being a mean person at all, in fact, he was quite cheerful and witty. But being fun wasn't part of his deliverables for the job. The company eventually got tired and parted ways with Lex. It wasn't just his poor work ethic on the assigned project with Lindiwe that hastened his departure. It was a sum of little things that could be summarized as a significant lack of self-discipline.

THE ART OF SELF-DISCIPLINE

Discipline isn't one thing; it's a set of small things you do over time. Self-discipline is the ability to power through discomfort in order to accomplish things even when you don't want to. It's sacrificing instant gratification for long-term gains. We often confuse self-discipline with motivation, but they are not the same. Motivation is the desire to undertake a specific goal. On the other hand, self-discipline is the drive and capacity to do what it takes to stick with the plan even on days when you lack motivation. Besides taking responsibility for my life, the next most crucial thing that I had to master was self-discipline. Like many people, I couldn't bring myself to persist with tasks and goals. As Stephen R. Covey said, "The undisciplined are slaves to moods, appetites, and passions." Are you?

Among us are talented, intelligent people yet they're unable to move forward. They are astonished when they see people with less pedigree who can accomplish incredible feats and take advantage of more opportunities in life. Why? I believe it comes primarily down to self-discipline. What about you? Do you identify with any of the statements below?

- You are inconsistent.
- You easily fall victim to temptations as you're led by your senses.
- You tend to do first and think later.
- You don't follow through with plans, ideas and tasks.
- You're unable to keep the promises you make.
- You tend to be everywhere but nowhere.

Self-discipline is essential for success in life. The inability to develop that capacity could lead to your failure, considering the hyperactive, always-connected and temptation-filled world we're in.

WHY DO YOU NEED SELF-DISCIPLINE?

You know the old adage that states "opportunity meets preparation"? That preparation is self-discipline. Whether in our professional or personal life, most of us usually want more options. "If only I had the chance," is a song many of us sing. But then when the opportunity shows up, not only don't we recognize it, we don't seize it. How so? We were never ready for it, that's why. We don't want to move out of our comfort zone. We struggle to put aside short-term gratification for long-term gains. Our feelings get the better of us. We complain about the state of things without taking the time to look within and make the necessary changes. That approach is dangerous and lethal.

Nurturing self-discipline is crucial for:

Progress

As David Allen remarked, "You can do anything but not everything." That's honestly the most straightforward way of saying, "Know your priorities and work on those, else it will cost you." Economists explain this well through the concept of opportunity cost: you have to give up something to obtain something else. Want to watch a movie? You give up time and money you could spend somewhere else. Want to become the best athlete? In addition to your natural talents, you have to train more, which may mean less time socializing. Having self-discipline helps you decide which costs you are willing to pay. Most successful people didn't become successful by doing everything. They followed through on their decisions and actions till they reached their goals.

Mental toughness

Being disciplined helps you withstand setbacks and disappointments. Even when you are giving and doing your best, you're bound to encounter challenges. Self-discipline will help you get over these, and you'll recognize the temporary nature of hardships and forge ahead from there.

Overall success

What's the secret to success? If you're continually working, hustling and doing everything yet without any results, take some time to re-evaluate your approach. According to Warren Buffett, one of the richest people on the planet, it's not about being smarter than other people but being more self-disciplined than anyone else. This applies to success in all aspects of your life.

Being more disciplined is undoubtedly the key to a prosperous life. Still, that doesn't mean that you will lead a restrictive life and have to follow a boring routine to the point of no longer having joy. On the contrary, being disciplined means that you will have a better sense of your priorities and follow-through in your choices. Your options today set the stage for the future you will have tomorrow. For the lifestyle you want, you have to give up something right here, right now.

STRENGTHENING YOUR SELF-DISCIPLINE

Think about what your life would be like if you consistently waltzed past discomfort and committed to doing what it takes to reach your potential. What would you accomplish? How far could you go? No one is born with an acquired sense of self-discipline as it's rather an intentional practice that requires patience and time. Time is an essential factor here. If you haven't been disciplined in your life until now, you won't wake up tomorrow and be the most disciplined person ever.

On your journey to strengthening your self-control muscle, you mustn't feel guilt, shame and blame yourself for moments that may arise when you fall off. You want to become sturdier, not develop self-hate nor dig your self-esteem into the ground. In addition, don't be shy to reach out. Enlist whoever can help you stay accountable to yourself and assist you in areas you're struggling with. Sometimes you may need to rely on external hands—this could be a coach, a therapist or a trainer to support you through the changes you seek in your life. Just do it! All the successful people you know who have accomplished tremendous things in life have developed self-discipline over time through repetition. Some of them may have done it alone, some may have had help. In the end, self-discipline is like a muscle—the more you exercise it, the more you will strengthen it. And you can do it, too!

Consider the following ideas to help you develop your self-discipline:

IN ACTION: BUILDING SELF-DISCIPLINE	
Instead of:	**Consider this:**
Belittling yourself for your lack of discipline.	**Self-acceptance** can help you become more disciplined.
Demonstrating a lack of focus.	**Define clear goals** and objectives in all areas of your life. Make them visible!
Being led by your emotions, feelings and easily falling prey to temptations.	**Remove temptations** from your environment. Temptations adversely impacts performance, so create a space that is line with your goals
Living in chaos.	**Get organized:** an organized life will lead to a disciplined life.

BOLDER TIP

With

BRIAN TRACY

What could be the secret to success? According to well-known author, speaker and coach Brian Tracy, there are nine disciplines you need to adopt if you want to be successful. They are:

1. **Clear thinking:** indulge in quiet time so you can think clearly.

2. **Daily goal setting:** know what you want out of life and set a daily goal around it. You'll be amazed by what a difference this makes.

3. **Effective time management:** aim to write your plans for tomorrow the night before. It will save you time and energy.

4. **Courage:** remind yourself daily of the limitless possibilities that abound around you. Use the mantra "I can do it" daily.

5. **Excellent health patterns:** a healthy mind and body creates a healthy life. Taking care of yourself is a way of demonstrating self-discipline.

6. **Saving and investing:** get into the habit of saving and not just spending.

7. **Hard work:** do the most important work first. Limit your distractions. Always try to start earlier than most people.

8. **Continuous learning:** don't become comfortable. Always strive to improve your knowledge and skills.

9. **Persistence:** this is the key to being self-disciplined. No matter what happens, just keep going!

A BOLDER YOU

In Action

SELF-DISCIPLINE

You know you could benefit from having better self-discipline, but you don't know where to start and how to go about it. Today's exercise is an invitation to embrace taking small steps towards the discipline you want. Let's start:

- **Pick an area** in your life right now where your discipline is at its lowest. It could be health, relationships, career etc.

- **Pinpoint one thing** within the category where you want to build more self-discipline. For example, let's say you tend to start playing with your phone as soon as you wake up. You now decide to go for a walk instead.

- **Ask yourself questions** relating to the change you want to see. In this case, it will be questions like:

  o What time should I go to bed in order to wake up earlier every morning?

  o Where should I leave all my devices so I'm not tempted? (removing temptations is important)

  o Who can hold me accountable?

- **Turn your answers to the questions above** into actionable steps that you can start taking. In this case, you could decide to go to bed by 9 p.m. or leave your phone in the living room. You could also buy an alarm clock and ask a friend or family member to hold you accountable.

- **Once you repeat** the same actions several times, it will be easier to keep going. Don't give up even if you fail a few times. Practice makes perfect.

- **Reward yourself.** As you build self-discipline in one area, make sure to take stock of your progress and take time to reward yourself!

CHAPTER 20

Building Systems For Your Life

——

"Everyone wants the same thing: to be happy, to be free,

to win. But whoever has the better system wins the prize."

—W. EDWARDS DEMING

Have you ever heard of army ants?

No, it's not the name of a boy band. Even though I have seen some pretty interesting names for boy bands over the years: Dogs Die in Hot Cars, Bathtub Shitter, Diarrhea Planet. I'm not making this stuff up! Don't believe me? Check for yourself, there's a whole thread on the Internet about the worst boy band names ever. Anyway.

No, I'm talking about a different kind of army ants here. These are carnivorous, nomadic insects that usually live in tropical areas. An army of raiders and hunters, these small ants are notorious for destroying the animal and plant life they meet on their path. As I discovered more about the species, what was fascinating to me is that a single colony of army ants—comprised of a queen, soldiers, workers, and young offspring—can capture 30,000 prey in just one day! Talk about an efficient and deadly system! As a business strategist, I have heard all about organizational and work systems. Who knew that even tiny creatures like ants have a system in place to live their best lives?

WHAT'S IN A SYSTEM?

The dictionary definition of the word system is "a collection of elements or components that are organized for a common purpose." Having a system makes things simpler. There's a reason why things work best when there's a structure. Imagine if every day something as trivial as your house's heating system needed to change. Every day, you'd have to wake up and put a new process in place for your heater to work. What a nightmare that would be! For businesses, systems are at the heart of their operations. One of the world's most recognized systems, Toyota's "Just in Time" manufacturing philosophy, helped the automaker and many other companies eliminate waste, improve responsiveness and become immensely successful. Can you imagine a business without organization? I can't even fathom the chaos they will have to contend with. And, as we know, even our world functions as a system. We often hear people refer to the "world system", a term coined by Immanuel Wallerstein to convey the notion of a system that forms a world, one that transcends political and cultural boundaries. So, what's your system?

THE SYSTEMS IN YOUR LIFE

If you're shaking your head in disagreement and think that you don't have a system, think again. Whether you realize it or not, we all have systems operating in our lives. You have one for shopping, one for paying bills and even one for planning vacations. And yes, even a lack of a system would still be considered a system! And that's where the problem lies for most of us. We tend to smash together various methods and tools that we copied from everywhere and everyone. We randomly throw them together and allow them to steer our lives. But all that does is set us back instead of empowering us to achieve our goals and move forward. You know why? Because we've never taken the time to ask ourselves if the way we are doing things is aligned with the goals we want to accomplish. We are just going at it blindly. We forget to reassess why and how we do things.

Have you thought that there could be a better way? The best way to do something is not how your friends or family members do it. It has to be linked to your goals and to the lifestyle you want. You need to consider adopting better systems in your life if:

- You are continually wasting your energy moving from one task to the next.

- You battle with interruptions and can't seem to finish your tasks.

- You lack focus on your priorities.

- You're prone to overthinking things, leading to indecisiveness.

- You're overwhelmed by a series of small problems that shouldn't be there in the first place.

SYSTEMS: THE GAME CHANGER

Overcoming procrastination is a must. Setting goals is necessary, but building personal systems in your life? That's the game-changer.

A goal without systems is like an engine without fuel.

I like to think about systems as ways of doing things to save us time and energy, making us more efficient and effective. In short, automated working processes. Winners and losers both want the same thing, but the former are the ones with better systems. Being victorious in life is not about luck, it's more than just hard work and fighting for your dreams. It's even more than merely setting goals. It's about the systems in your life.

Goals are useful for planning your progress. Systems are suitable for making progress.

—JAMES CLEAR

Most well-known successful people keep prospering not only because of the goals they set but mostly because of the systems they follow. For example, consider Albert Einstein, who was photographed consistently wearing a gray suit. Steve Jobs, in his black turtleneck and Mark Zuckerberg always rocking a gray T-shirt. Instead of spending time on a bunch of small decisions related to clothing on a daily basis, these individuals put in place a system for their wardrobe. Famous people aside, you may have encountered successful people who inspire you by the way they approach life. My friend Willy is one of those. An accomplished entrepreneur, he always seems to float from one challenge to the next, taking them on without seemingly breaking a sweat. I've always been intrigued by how he does it. When most of us are left disheveled by running from one task to the next, he always seems to remain composed and stay on top of things. One of the conversations I had with him about his methodology convinced me to include this chapter. As he likes to say, "Your attitude may determine your altitude, but a sound system lowers your stress." The systems you implement in your life should make life simpler and give you more clarity and control. You want systems that will work for you, not against you. Building personal systems gives you the freedom and the energy to live purposefully instead of living restrained.

BUILDING WINNING SYSTEMS

Personal systems are what give wings to your goals. If you want your dreams to materialize, you have to establish a certain structure that will help you build momentum when your motivation no longer drives you. The two crucial elements of a successful system are your rituals and habits. In writing this book, I had to find a system that would help me reach my publishing goal. Mine was a ritual of accomplishing at least two pages worth of writing every single evening, essentially making a habit out of it. It wasn't a question of "if I feel like it" or "if time allows."

Now, time for you to do the same and build personal systems that will work best in your life and for your life. Consider the following:

IN ACTION: BUILDING PERSONAL SYSTEMS

Instead of:	Consider this:
Wasting energy from one task to the next by thinking what you should do	**Evaluate the current systems in your life**. Do an audit within each category of your life to determine what's working and what isn't.
Lacking focus.	**Ask yourself what you want the system to do for you.** Knowing the outcome you expect from your system will help you adopt the right process. Do you want to exercise more often or do you want to exercise more efficiently? This question could lead to different systems.

BOLDER TIP

With

JANE TAYLOR

Before we get started on our exercise for the day, here are some great tips from the founder of *Habits for Wellbeing* Jane Taylor on how to go about building systems in your life:

- **Be clear on what you want to systemize:** you have to know what area of your life could benefit from a system.

- **The why of the system:** figure out why you need to have a system in that particular area. Start by clarifying your purpose.

- **Determine the "how" of the system:** make sure to determine the fundamentals and non-essentials to progress with your system.

- **Find the needs:** what are the resources (human and physical) you need to complete the system.

- **Review:** commit to reviewing and monitoring your progress. Don't lose track of the changes that the system is bringing to your life.

A BOLDER YOU

In Action

DESIGNING A SYSTEM FOR YOUR LIFE

For today's exercise, you'll spend time designing a system in areas of your life where you think you need improvement.

STEP 1:

Pick an activity you'd like to improve on in any area of your life and where you think you could benefit from having a system. For example, it could be that you want to have a better system for your meal preparation or getting ready for bed. Write down the activity that needs to be improved.

STEP 2:

After choosing the activity, answer these five questions:

- How am I currently getting this activity done?

- What frustrates me about this activity?

- Are all the steps I'm taking to do this activity necessary? If not, how can I make this activity better and more effective?

- Do I need to keep a checklist? Do I need to write on a board? Will keeping a visual help to do the activity better?

- What's the ultimate result/outcome you would like to see with the new system?

STEP 3:

Now that you've reviewed how you currently do your activity and have pinpointed where you need to change, it's time to plan the system for your activity.

- Write down a series of steps that you would like to keep for your activity.

- Add additional steps that you think are missing and could help make your system better.

- Enumerate and arrange all of the above in the correct order.

Execute your plan and put it to the test. The key is to keep using it and to Monitor your progress to ensure that your system keeps delivering results for your life.

BETTER

//To be more effective, to increase the good qualities

—

From "good to great" is the anthem for the last leg of the journey.

Together, we're going to learn how to use an array of tools that you can arm yourself with for self-betterment.

Our time here will be spent on practical and achievable strategies that you can harness to build your network, establish self-advocacy and practice gratitude — all for the life-changing improvements you are soon to experience.

Ready?

CHAPTER 21

Fail Forward

"You build on failure. You use it as a stepping stone. Close

the door to the past. You don't try to forget the mistakes.

But you don't dwell on it. You don't let it have your energy

or any of your time, or any of your space."

—JOHNNY CASH

The best is yet to come.

"Are you there? Can you hear me?" Enyonam asked me over the phone. Laying down on my couch, trying hard to hold back my tears, I wanted to hang up. Even though I needed to hear Eny's reaffirming and uplifting voice more than ever, I also wanted to disappear and forget about all the turmoil I was going through.

"Yes...I am here," I replied. "Don't worry, things will get better" she said. "Rejection is redirection, you know. And the best is yet to come." The last three words pushed me over the edge. I had enough. I needed to get some air. "Hum...I will call you back, okay?" I said, barely holding back my tears while I quickly ended the phone call.

As long as I've known Eny, as I affectionately call her, "the best is yet to come" has been her mantra. No matter the trials and tribulations she's experienced in her life, she's always lived by that philosophy. We often joke that if "the best is yet to come" was a person, it will probably be her. A woman of faith and courage, I could always count on her. Through her warmth and poise, she always knew exactly how to bring the people in her circle out of the depths of despair they would find themselves in.

And at that particular moment, I was swimming in an ocean of misery. Out of the five top graduate schools I applied to, none accepted me. I didn't see it coming. There was no interview request or even a shortlist option, I was flat-out denied. I felt the heat. The degree of my failure was like a stinging hot burn that is still vivid in my mind, even though I can now laugh about it. Have you ever been in a situation where you are so sure of something? You've done all the mathematical calculations in your mind about how success was guaranteed? That was me. I had performed every scenario analysis that could show me the path to acceptance to one of these top schools. Rejection was not on the cards and yet it happened. I didn't have time to hold my breath. It was one rejection after the other. How could that be? I was shell-shocked and angry. But as Eny reminded me, I still had other choices. The thing is I didn't want other choices. There was no option B in my mind. I was adamant that it would have to be option A or nothing.

It was all a disaster. I had already publicized to my friends and colleagues that I was going to a famous graduate school. I had sold my car, gave notice at my job and started clearing out my apartment. It's often said that to truly manifest something, you have to fully live it out. "Walk in faith," they say. Here I just didn't walk, I sprinted! Yet the only thing I manifested was failure. And failure was nowhere in my scenario planning but it soon became part of my reality. None of us want to fail because we all glorify success. We hear and read stories about inspiring people, and rightfully, we want to be just like them— maybe even better. Our societies only celebrate winners, losers are quickly forgotten and drowned out in a sea of applause. But amid our obsession with triumph, we tend to overlook the many attempts that these successful people may have gone through. We all know the adage that Rome wasn't built in a day, and that it takes time to build something solid and long lasting. So why do we harbor failure so much?

FEAR OF FAILURE

Failure is defined as the state or condition of not meeting a desirable or intended objective. Of all the definitions I came across, I particularly liked this one because of the word "state". State means that it's temporary, it can change. It also means that it's something outside of you. It's not who you are, and it's not who you will be. Yet, we tend to fear trying anything new because the outcome might be negative. How many of these statements do you identify with?

- You worry about what people think of you.

- You worry that if you fail, people will no longer consider you.

- You worry about failure because you don't feel capable.

- You always tell people that you will fail before starting to mitigate expectations.

- You tend to procrastinate and don't get started on anything.

- You worry that you'll disappoint the people in your life.

If any, or all, of these statements resonate with you, you are not alone. Most of us fear failure, and we do so for a variety of reasons:

Education

If you've been raised by critical people or spent time a lot of time with them, it's likely that you would have developed a fear of failure (and other insecurities) from them. You've probably internalized all that you've heard, and now they're stopping you from trying new things.

Fear of shame

We are afraid of being embarrassed, and we want to avoid the pain that could come from risk-taking, so we just don't get out of our comfort zones.

Fear of rejection

We want acceptance and we desire to belong. That's natural as we are born like that. We harbor failure because we don't want to be judged as inadequate, nor do we want to be excluded from our social groups.

Loss aversion

Nobel prize winners Daniel Kahneman and Amos Tversky explained that in most cases we would place a higher value on avoiding losses than on potential gains. Loss aversion is mistaken as risk aversion.

Taking criticism personally

We fear failure because we care a lot about what other people think. Criticism can be crushing and can make us feel unworthy, so we stay away from anything that could allow us to hear even the slightest of judgments.

All these and more could be the underlying reasons why we fear failure so much. However, if you don't try at all you'll never know what you're missing out on. It's certain that the road to success is not paved with gold, but you might find a treasure pot at the end.

FAILURE IS NOT FINAL

Do you know how many times Edison, who discovered the light bulb, failed before succeeding? How about Walt Disney? JK Rowling, author of the Harry Potter series? Ever heard about how Colonel Sanders, who launched Kentucky Fried Chicken (KFC) at the ripe old age of

62, was rejected by no less than 1,009 people before making headway with his idea? These individuals failed again and again, but eventually, they positively impacted our society in their respective fields. Today, we enjoy and reap the fruits of their perseverance. Imagine if they had given up at their first, second or even hundredth attempt.

Failure is not fatal, and the myth of overnight success is nothing but a legend. At every stage of your life you'll encounter disappointments and misadventures. You will be criticized for daring to try. You are bound to stumble and fall. That's okay. How do you think it became possible for you to walk properly without first wobbling and falling over? How you handle failure will help you prepare for the next levels to come, or else you'll be taken out of the game altogether. Your perspective about it will determine your progress. A delay in growth is not a flat-out denial of success. Failure, in many cases, comes bearing lessons and new ideas. Am I saying that your defeats can be positive? Absolutely. It all depends on how one looks at it:

Failure is a teacher

Failure has a way of sending us messages. Sometimes it's merely saying "not right now" or "try again". Other times it wants to let us know that we are not adequately prepared, that we need to gain more skills. When you fail, as painful as it can be, there is an opportunity to learn, pivot and take another direction. The lessons you picked up from your failure are never lost. They can be used to set you on a different—and potentially better—path.

Failure is a character builder

You don't become mentally strong by sailing smoothly through life. Failing establishes your strength, resilience and fortitude. You learn to appreciate the best when you have been through the worst. Every error enables you to prepare for the next level in life. So instead of crumbling like a sandcastle, you'll be able to stand your ground, back yourself up and move forward.

Failure is an inspiration

Failure can inspire you to introspect and discover new, better ways to approach life. When you face rejection, instead of taking it as an indictment on your inability to perform, ask yourself: "What am I missing out in this situation?" Failure can reveal the secret ingredient for your breakthrough, so take the time to find it.

Successful people become experts in failure. They understand that all of their rejection stories, deferred dreams and missed goals will eventually lead them to the place they want to be. They embrace failure as a requirement for victory and permit themselves to make mistakes. Perhaps we should stop referring to them as "successful people" but rather "conquerors." After all, they worked their way to the top by bravely overcoming the steep ladders.

PERMISSION TO FAIL

"When we give ourselves permission to fail, we, at the same time, give ourselves permission to excel."

—ELOISE RISTAD

Are you permitting yourself to fail? Failing is human, but it should not define you. It's vital to separate yourself from your failures and make peace with them. Too often, we hold on to failures as if they are flaws in our character, holding us back from unleashing our true selves and achieving our goals. Permitting yourself to fail is about knowing that something might not work out but attempting to do it anyway as a learning process. Allowing yourself to be vulnerable is about acknowledging that you may not be the most qualified candidate but confidently applying for that job regardless. It's about realizing that you might not finish the marathon, yet training hard to compete against the professionals. You don't need a million "yeses". You may have thousands of failures, but it could only take one small win to unlock success. Keep on going!

Are you permitting yourself to excel? Some of us haven't discovered what success really means, and our definition of failure is based on influences from the world engulfing us. Trying to live up to society's version of success will always make you feel like a loser. Comparison is destructive, after all. If you don't establish your personal purpose, you won't know your standards for what victory should consist of. If you keep blindly following through what they say you should do, you won't discover ways to excel on your own, beautiful way. The best way to give yourself permission to fail is by coming up with a personal definition for failure. Above all, remember that a failure right now could be a stepping stone to success.

Here are some tips to consider when you experience failure:

IN ACTION: FAIL FORWARD	
Instead of:	**Consider this:**
Denying how you feel about the failures you experienced.	**Allow yourself to deeply feel the emotions** stemming from the failure. But don't dwell on it either. Don't make it personal. Failure is something that happens. It's not who you are.
Letting fear of failure hold you hostage and stop you from trying new things.	**List all the things that could go wrong** if you fail at what you're attempting to do. Facing that list doesn't mean the failure won't come, but at least you would have explored the potential worst case scenarios.
Seeing failure as final.	**Reframe what you see.** Start seeing failure as feedback. Ask yourself what the failure is trying to teach you. What good could come out of this? Write it down as it will help you to process it.
Disregarding what failure is trying to show you.	**Keep learning.** Failure gives us messages and also shows us where we have gaps. Stay curious and learn what you can to fill the gaps.

BETTER STORY

With

JACK MA

You've heard of Facebook, Amazon and eBay but have you heard of Alibaba? And as much as there's a lot to be said about Alibaba, China's biggest ecommerce company, I want to focus on the story of its founder Jack Ma. His story is often told as a rags-to-riches one but it's really a story of resilience, patience and persistence in overcoming and embracing failure. Rising from a humble background, Jack Ma is now a self-made tech billionaire and the richest man in China.

But it was no smooth ride for Ma. From his education to the business world, Ma encountered numerous failures. He failed three times in primary school and twice in secondary school. Ma was rejected by Harvard University a whopping ten times! He eventually graduated as an English major. After this, he tried to get a job and was rejected by all thirty organizations he applied to. He even applied for a job at Kentucky Fried Chicken (KFC)—Ma was the only one rejected in the group of twenty five applicants. He then applied to be a police officer, and among a mere five candidates he was once again rejected. Before launching Alibaba, Ma failed at two other ventures. And even with Alibaba, there were several times where the company was on the verge of bankruptcy.

These failures may have been devastating but he never paused even for a bit, nor did he give up. That made all the difference. As he stated, "If you don't give up, you still have a chance. Giving up is the greatest failure."

Try again.

A BETTER YOU

In Action

WHAT'S THE WORST THAT COULD HAPPEN?

You are about to start a new venture, a new career or make a move but you are paralyzed by a fear of failure. You keep thinking how your decision could be a mistake, you spend days wondering about people's criticisms if you fail. Yes, failure is possible, just like anything is. A defeat could be bad but it could also be amazingly life-changing. Instead of talking yourself out of trying, why not just face your fear? Rather than quitting to explore an idea or a move you're contemplating, ask yourself: "What is the worst thing that could happen?" But don't keep all the answers in your mind.

Today's exercise, inspired by Tim Ferris, will help you explore this question and work through it in five steps:

Step 1: draw a table and divide it into three columns.

Step 2: in the first column labeled "Fear," write down your fear(s) and what you think could go wrong.

Step 3: in the second column labeled "Limit," think about what you could do to minimize the damage for each fear scenario.

Step 4: in the last column labeled "Fix," list the ways that could repair the effects should your worst fear materialize.

Step 5: based on the above, rate each listed fear from 1 (minimal impact) to 10 (life-changing impact).

Putting all your fears down and rating them will help you move forward in a better way. By seeing all the ways you can limit or fix potential failures, you could easily finalize decisions. I have provided a completed example of this exercise in the resources section.

CHAPTER 22

Focus

—

*"I don't care how much power, brilliance or energy you
have, if you don't harness it and focus it on a specific
target, and hold it there, you're never going to accomplish
as much as your ability warrants."*

—ZIG ZIGLAR

FOMO.

FOMO means the "Fear of Missing Out" and even though you may not be familiar with the term, you've probably experienced it. Whether we want to admit it or not, we've all been guilty of following that mindset at some point.

In short, FOMO is the anxiety that arises due to social exclusion or isolation, particularly in the context of social media. It's triggered by watching what other people are doing and posting, and is characterized by experiencing intense feelings of self-doubt mixed with inadequacy because you are not included in those special moments. FOMO is unhealthy and irrational because it pushes you to think that everyone is having more fun than you are, even when you're on the right track. With FOMO looming over your head like a dark cloud, you're focused on the colorful things others are doing instead of focusing on what is most important in your own life. FOMO leads us to stray from a minimalist yet goal-oriented life: we spend more and save less because of the latest fads that will soon be replaced by new ones. We waste time catching up with the latest technology, so we lose energy for the most genuine connections that matter. In short, we direct our focus onto something unworthy and so we get stuck.

BE COMFORTABLE WITH MISSING OUT

We know it's physically, mentally and emotionally impossible to be everywhere, so why do you feel like you should? There's always something that you will miss out on. Each decision and action you take in your life will cost you something. Instead of feeling left out and stressing over what everyone may be enjoying, it's necessary to be okay with focusing on your own joys if you truly desire legitimate progress. The antidote to FOMO is JOMO, which means the "Joy of Missing Out". With JOMO, you're more intentional, more comfortable with your own affairs and embrace what really matters most instead of trying to "keep up with the Joneses".

Your momentum is hijacked every day, and you are assailed with an onslaught of requests, activities and obligations. Everything and everyone is vying for your attention. Unless you stay on top of all the things coming your way, your journey to self-betterment will get interrupted. Being scattered will bring you just that—crumbles, pieces here and there that won't amount to anything substantive. The more distractions you can remove from your life, the better you'll fare. You have to protect your attention and give life only to what will add meaning and value. Your engagement is a valuable currency that you must protect at all costs. Your awareness will determine the type of results that you'll get. Do you relate to any of the following?

- You tend to drift from idea to idea.
- You quickly get driven by other people's priorities.
- You tend to say "yes" to every opportunity that calls your name.
- You do a lot but don't see any results.
- You struggle with making decisions.

There is no shortage of distractions in life. Surely, we can blame the Internet and new technology for the volume of noise we're subjected to. But if we aspire to get observable results towards achieving our goals, then we must adopt radical focus by saying "good bye" to FOMO and "hello" to JOMO!

THE NEED FOR RADICAL FOCUS

"I think you are spreading yourself thin," Shingai said as she ended her telephonic coaching session with one of her clients. As long as I've known Shingai she has consistently shared the same message: "You can't do everything at once." Her coaching audience was primarily scattered small business owners who tend to have a different idea they want to pursue every other day of the week. They always seemed to be chasing what's currently "in" and believing that this fad would be better than the last. We often find ourselves falling into these traps ourselves by going after too many things. Soon enough, we are jacks of all trades yet masters of none. Unless you give yourself the gift of being radically focused in your life, success will always be a mirage. By being focused, you can:

Give your best and be your best

There is beauty in doing less. The less you do, the higher quality of work you can produce. It's a case of quality over quantity, again and again.

Less stress

When your focus is crystal clear, your mind and body will thank you. Radical focus helps you create structure in your life. Where there is chaos, there is stress. Where there is stress, nothing grows.

Gain Mastery

If you want to master just about anything, you need to invest in focus, consistency and patience. We admire successful people because of their expertise, but we fail to adopt their unrivaled attention span.

Imagine if Tiger Woods decided to be a pro golfer, a pro tennis player and a pro basketball player all at the same time. He would have failed, and we would have never seen his prowess play out on the golf course. He embraced his natural talents and doubled down his focus to become a master in this craft.

MASTERING YOUR FOCUS

In our modern age, we have diverse options and opportunities, and we get tempted to do everything at the same time. We're told that we should never put all our eggs in one basket, we need to have a variety of tricks. Why so? They say it's because nothing is guaranteed. We have to be ready for another thing if this one fails.

I disagree. To quote Andrew Carnegie: "Put all your eggs in one basket, and then watch that basket. Look round you and take notice; men who do that do not often fail." Truth is, we are often inspired by men and women who followed Carnegie's advice. We are inclined to hire and trust people who master one thing. For our teeth, we go to a dentist, not a generalist. If we struggle with our taxes, we call an accredited tax practitioner. We tend to put our trust in people who have a single focus, who are working according to their niche. This doesn't mean you can't have many interests, but you should focus on one at a time. You can have a desire to learn new skills but start with the most accessible for now. You may want to plan many vacations but focus on the first one. Once you start focusing and going with one thing at the time, you will soon become unstoppable.

Here are some tips to help you focus better:

IN ACTION: FOCUS

Instead of:	Consider this:
Spending time trying to multitask.	**Adopt the practice of focusing** on one thing at a time.
Easily giving your time away to everything.	**Improve your time management** with techniques to help you take control of your schedule.
Giving way to distractions and other people's agendas.	**Set your goals and** make sure they are visible so you don't lose track of them.
Feeling depleted.	**Reduce stress** by taking care of your mental and physical health. Self-care matters.

BETTER TIP

With

GARY KELLER AND JAY PAPASAN

What if I tell you that you can achieve anything if you focus on only one thing? Yes, just one. It sounds simple yet it could bring profound changes to your life.

Gary Keller and Jay Papasan are the authors behind the groundbreaking book *The ONE Thing* and what they have labelled as the "Focusing Question". Essentially, Keller and Papasan believe that everything in our life comes down to the questions we ask ourselves. So, if we want to live fulfilling and extraordinary lives, it's important that we learn how to ask ourselves good questions.

The Focusing Question goes like this:

> *"What is the ONE thing I can do such that by doing it everything else will be easier or unnecessary?"*

In other words, what is the one thing you can do to move the needle forward? What this question does is push you to not only choose a single thing but also one that you can work with now, not tomorrow or in the near future. This question pushes you to rank and prioritize. There are many wonderful things you could do for sure. But find the one thing that will start the chain reaction needed to make progress right at this very instant because in the end, it's not about doing everything but the most appropriate thing.

A BETTER YOU

In Action

YOUR ONE THING

For today's exercise, I want us to work with the concept of the focusing question by Keller and Papasan. There's a lot we can get out of this question if we apply it to various categories in our lives. This will be a reflection exercise and this is how you should go about it:

STEP 1:

List all the areas of your life that matter to you, for example—

- Relationships

- Career

- Health

- Personal development

- Socializing

- Others (you can add any other category that you may deem relevant in your life)

STEP 2:

For each category, ask yourself the focusing question. Formulate it like this: For "category" + what is the one thing I can do to _____ + (insert your goal and time frame) such that by doing it everything will be easier or unnecessary?

For example, in the category of relationships, if I'm trying to make new friends, a question I could ask myself might be: "For relationships, what's the one thing I can do to make new friends by the first quarter of the year such that by doing it everything will be easier?"

STEP 3:

Once you have the clarity you seek from the question, don't stop there. Act on it! Make a habit of asking yourself this question as often as possible. It will help light the path forward. I use this question every time I feel stuck and don't know where to go and what to do.

Try it!

CHAPTER 23

Find Your Strengths

—

"Focus on your strengths instead of your weaknesses, on your powers instead of your problems."

—PAUL MEYERS

One of the most traditional interview questions has to be, "What is your greatest weakness?" It's a tricky and a terrible one, if you ask me, but its popularity remains.

Think about it. If you reply to this question by saying that you have no weakness, you are deemed to lack awareness. If you do decide to acknowledge one of your shortcomings, you also have to tread lightly. In fact, many career coaches recommend that you do it in a way where you are not oversharing but still will resonate with your future employer. Some career specialists go as far as recommending that you take stock of your flaws and put a list together for when the question comes up in interviews. There is so much focus on improving on our weaknesses and not enough on playing to our strengths. If anything, that's what we should amplify.

YOUR STRENGTHS MATTER

What makes you feel strong and what makes you feel weak—that's how Marcus Buckingham defines strength and weakness. There are various definitions to these words but Buckingham's versions truly resonated with me. As he puts it, "A strength is not what you are good at and a weakness is not what you are bad at." Instead, Buckingham invites us to see the former as something that empowers us and the latter as something that drains us, even if you're good at it! For example, you could be efficient in managing projects, but if every time you do it you feel drained afterwards then it's a weakness not a strength.

We all have strengths! Yes, you do, even though you may not have zoned in into them yet. But before we go any further, there's also the confusion around strengths, talents and skills that we need to clarify. See, we often confuse strengths with talents. They are not the same but are also not mutually exclusive. A talent is something that comes naturally to you, while a strength is an ability that you've developed over time. So, what's the link between talents and strengths? Strengths are talents refined.

Your talents get you in the race.

Your strengths take you to the finish line.

Talents don't tell us the whole story, and the reality is that simply having them is not enough. No successful person has ever relied on talents alone as they don't guarantee success at all. If you want to soar, you need the perfect combination of talents and strengths, coupled with relevant skills or abilities that you gain from knowledge and repetition. Because we obsess over avoiding failures, we look for gaps to fill. We're afraid of not being enough, so our focus tends to be on what's wrong with us rather than what's great about us. But by making weaknesses the center of our attention, all we do is become drained and before you know it we lose confidence. Do any of these sound familiar?

- You can easily list your weaknesses but don't know any of your strengths.

- You're envious of other people's strengths and think you've lost out on that front.

- You're caught up in the rat race and are always comparing yourself to others.

- You procrastinate.

If you relate to any of these statements and realize that it's time for a change, you might want to adopt a strengths-based strategy.

A STRENGTHS-BASED STRATEGY

Various studies have shown that people who spend time embracing their strengths are more confident, healthier and happier in their lives. Adopting a strengths-based strategy is all about investing in your positive attributes rather than your weaknesses. It's about acknowledging that, like everyone, you have flaws. But that it's more worthwhile to enhance what you're good at than going on and on about your weaknesses.

The Pareto principle, also known as the "80/20 rule", suggests that 80% of our results will come from only about 20% of our efforts and activities. Applying this to a strengths-based strategy means that you should focus on the 20% that you do best. If 20% of your strengths can add 80% of value and results, imagine what glory you could achieve if you nurture and give more attention to them. By adopting this technique in your life, you'll not only make strengths stronger but will likely also realize the great potential that lies within. Fine-tuning your strengths will lead you to becoming the best version of yourself, thereby radically enhancing your self-worth.

The world is made up of a little bit of everything and different types of people are needed to make it go around. If we were all the same, how boring and predictable would that be? How would we even function? We need doctors, architects, chefs and all types of people for the world to work optimally. This is not to say that one should put blinders on, completely ignoring the reality of your flaws. What is essential is to be aware of weaknesses while not dwelling on them. Just take the time to delegate, and enlist help to deal with those areas where you're struggling.

IDENTIFY YOUR STRENGTHS

Discovering your strengths is not as straightforward as identifying your weaknesses. If I were to ask you about your weaknesses, you would probably list them rather quickly. This is due to the fact that they are usually linked to past events, mistakes or experiences that we suffered through, so we remember them more vividly.

In any case, here are some ideas to help you zone in on your strengths:

IN ACTION: FIND YOUR STRENGHTS	
Instead of:	**Consider this:**
Relying on others first to help identify your strengths.	**Take stock of your own strengths.** It will require introspection and reflection, but you can do it.
Spending your time zoning in on what you are not good at.	**Figure out what energizes you.** Know and name these things.
Being scattered and trying to adopt other people's strengths.	**Pay attention.** Life is usually talking to you. There are clues that life directly and indirectly has been sending you.
Playing the guessing game	**Take a self-assessment test** online or offline.
Randomly asking people who don't know you well.	**Tap into your trusted network.** Ask former colleagues, teammates and mentors to further your analysis. My recommendation is to only do this after you've taken stock of your own perceived strengths first. Do the work before asking others.

BETTER TIP

With

MARCUS BUCKINGHAM

How do you find your strengths? Who do you need to speak to? Where should one go?

According to Marcus Buckingham, an author, speaker and prominent researcher on strengths and leadership, it all starts with you. Yes, you! As mentioned previously, he believes that your strengths are those things you enjoy doing and boost you. It's not just about performance. You can excel greatly in an activity but if it drains you and you'd rather not do it, then it's not a strength. Ultimately, you are the best person to determine your strengths. A good way to do so is to use Buckingham's SIGN method:

- **Success:** look out for activities which you enjoy doing and excel at.

- **Instinct:** these are things that you instinctively gravitate towards.

- **Growth:** there is growth each time you perform those activities.

- **Needs:** you sense the need to get involved in these activities.

A BETTER YOU

In Action

FINDING YOUR STRENGTHS

For today's exercise, we'll be building on the work of Marcus Buckingham and his SIGN method. Ready to uncover your strengths? Here are the four key steps to take:

STEP 1:

Follow the SIGN acronym and write down answers to these questions:

- **S**uccess: what are the activities that you have undertaken this week and have energized you to the point of you being successful in them?

- **I**nstinct: what are the things that you naturally gravitated towards so far this week?

- **G**rowth: what are the activities which make you feel like you are growing or let you see some opportunities for growth?

- **N**eeds: what are the activities that may help you fulfill one of your core needs (variety, love, significance, connection, contribution, growth, certainty)?

STEP 2:

Summarize by listing all the tasks that you mentioned during the first step.

STEP 3:

Don't just stop there. Try to arrange your SIGNs into themes if you see some emerging. If you don't see any, that's fine too.

STEP 4:

Think about developing an action plan for your professional life around your SIGNs.

To complement this exercise, I strongly suggest you take the Gallup *Strengths Finder Assessment* available online. Also consider the *Reflected Best Self-Exercise* that will help you gather further feedback on strengths from outsiders. Check out the resources section for links.

CHAPTER 24

Find Your Why

—

"Having a purpose is the difference between making a

living and making a life."

—TOM THISS

What do you want to be when you grow up?

Ha! That awkward question adults like to ask children. As a child, I blurted out once that I wanted to be an archeologist. At eight years old, all I enjoyed was dressing fashionably and reading stories about Egyptian mummies and tomb raiders. I was enamored with the idea of being an archeologist until a well-meaning family friend destroyed it by saying that being one would be boring and that all the mummies' tombs had already been unearthed. I was wasting my brain cells dreaming of a path that would never materialize. Suffice to say, that conversation left the young child that I was utterly confused. I did not become an archeologist, and it took me years to eventually find my purpose. Such is the lasting impact of a seemingly meaningless conversation from a trusted adult to a child.

On the other hand, my sister Rockyath was boldly declaring to anyone who cared to listen that she was going to be a star from an early age. She went as far as doing a vision board of these words with some pictures to remind herself of her life purpose. Today, she is a star ... in other people's lives. Her life's purpose, as she explains it, is to help shine the light on the weak, the invisible and the forgotten within our society. She gets to live it out every day as an advocate and the founder of Auction for Change, an organization at the intersection of arts and social activism.

What about you? Have you found your purpose? So many of us ask ourselves this question, and it can take years—even decades—to find an answer. What's a purpose anyway?

THE MEANING OF PURPOSE

A purpose is not a job

We often confuse purpose with a job. The latter depends on external circumstances and is unreliable. One day, you have a job and the next you find yourself in the unemployment line. Purpose, on the contrary, is independent of your job title and the company you work for. In some cases, a job can be a conduit to living your purpose as in my sister's case. But not everyone gets to live their niche through their job. You might be thinking "Okay ... fine. So, what about passion? Isn't passion the equivalent of purpose?"

A purpose is not a passion

Passion and purpose are often used interchangeably, but they are not the same. Even though your passion is a gateway to your purpose, it's something you are enthusiastic about—it brings you contentment, energy and joy. And it's usually driven by your emotions.

A purpose is not for a select few

We're driven to believe that a purpose is a special calling only attainable by a chosen group of people. That's not true. You don't need to be a monk, a saint, nor a world-class athlete to be worthy of a purpose.

So, what's a purpose? "Purpose" is defined in the field of psychology as: "A stable and generalized intention to accomplish something that is at once personally meaningful and at the same times leads to productive engagement with some aspect of the world beyond the self." In summary, it can't be a selfish endeavor. It's fitting to say then that your purpose is what you love to do and what helps others. Your motivation and life's mission is directly linked to impact. Purpose is about direction and living out loud the following statement: how do I meaningfully use my gifts to impact others positively? Author Jay Shetty summed it up when he stated, "Your passion is for you, and your purpose is for others. When you use your passion in the service of others, it becomes your purpose."

THE WHY BEHIND YOUR WHY

As a society, we're fascinated with the concept of purpose. We buy books about it, watch movies on it and consume endless podcasts telling us how to find it. We know that finding our purpose won't miraculously resolve all the world's problems, but that doesn't stop us from fervently seeking it. Maybe it's because we see others living out their purpose and we become inspired to follow suit. Perhaps it's because the uncertainty gives us a weird sense of hopelessness. Do any of these apply to you?

- You're not excited about life and have nothing to look forward to.

- You're frustrated that your natural gifts are not being used.

- You feel like something is missing.

- You're aimless and adopt other people's goals.

- You're always looking for external approval.

If any of these statements resonate with you, you're in good company. Joining the search committee for unraveling what purpose means will lead you to feel alive and fulfilled. Above that, you will also gain:

Clarity

Knowing your purpose will keep you focused and make your life easier. You'll spend less energy and time on activities that are not aligned with who you are and what you want. You can have goals, but you are essentially walking in the dark if they are not aligned with your purpose.

Confidence

When you know your purpose, you'll be less prone to seek external validation. You'll become more confident with your choices and boldly go in the direction you desire.

Physical and mental health

Knowing your purpose is good for your health. There are various research studies that demonstrate how a more substantial and definite purpose in life might be associated with decreased mortality.

Resilience

In his research, Harvard Professor Jon Jachimowicz suggests that chasing purpose will make us more successful than going after passion. Because purpose will make you more resilient, this will sustain you in the long run, propelling you on the path to success.

FINDING YOUR PURPOSE

Finding your purpose is about being more of who you already are. We often think that we can only start living once we have discovered it. The truth is, our purpose is not separate from us, and therefore it doesn't require the development of a different persona. Being our authentic self is more than enough. We are also inclined to think that our purpose will come to us as a special delivery from the post office or through an epiphany—a grand revelation to guide us towards the promised land. It may happen in that way for some, but it's merely a journey of self-discovery for most of us. Seeking our reasons for living is a personal endeavor that is deliberate and intentional. While you don't need to stare at the sky, become a monk and go on a sabbatical trip around the world to find your purpose, you have to take the time to introspect and tune in to your inner voice to align your values with your passions. But finding your purpose is not the be-all and end-all. As Jennifer Benz said, "Purpose doesn't free you from working hard and being challenged, it will drive you to put yourself further out of your comfort zone. The falls will be harder, but the wins will feel so much better."

If you're ready to discover your purpose and live more fully, consider these options:

IN ACTION: FIND YOUR PURPOSE

Instead of:	Consider this:
Trying everything and anything in the hope of finding your purpose.	**Reflect on** what you love, what you are good at, what the world needs and what you can get paid for.
Adopting someone else's purpose because they seem to be having the time of their life.	**Visualize your best self.** Think through these questions: What are you doing? What is important to you? What do you really care about and why?
Looking externally for direction and a compass.	**Take a look at your values.** Your values are signposts towards your path. And because they drive you to be your authentic self, they can help you find your purpose.

Finding your life purpose doesn't have to be complicated. What if I told you there is a simple formula you could use? Sounds too good to be true, right? Richard Leider, one of America's most prominent executive life coaches, came up with the purpose formula. Leider has dedicated his life to help us discover and activate our innate motivations. What's in his purpose formula? And can one really find the answer to the reason for existence by using a pre-made structure? According to Leider, you can. The simple, yet powerful, formula is:

$$G + P + V = C$$

$$G(GIFTS) + P(PASSION) + V(VALUES) = C (CALLING)$$

You truly get to live your purpose every day in small and big ways when you combine these three elements: gifts, passions and values. Leider adds that:

- Gifts are what you enjoy doing and what you're good at.

- Your passion is what you are curious about and like to get involved in.

- Your environment should match the values you hold.

Above all, as Leider advises, stay curious about yourself and others. That's the key to becoming purposeful in everything you do.

A BETTER YOU

In Action

DISCOVER YOUR IKIGAI

Ikigai is a Japanese concept that dates back to the Heian period (794-1185). The word Ikigai is a combination of two words: "iki" which means "life" and "gai" meaning "reason" which together can be translated as "your purpose in life".

Think of Ikigai as the crossover of various points:

- **Passion:** things you love to do
- **Mission:** things the world needs
- **Profession:** things you are good at
- **Vocation:** things you can get paid for

It's about what brings you satisfaction and meaning. Finding your Ikigai is specific to you. After all, you can't copy someone else's purpose.

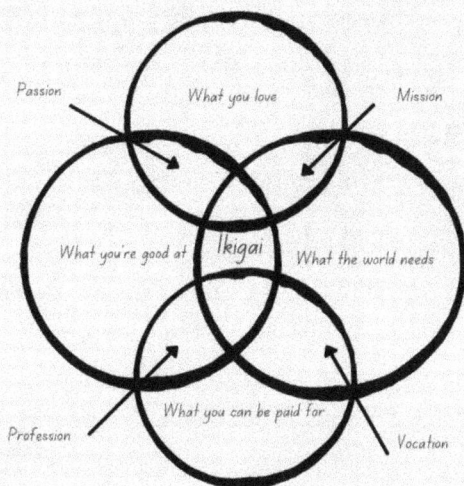

Ikigai is a great framework to explore your life's direction. There are various principles to follow in order to ensure that you live your Ikigai in the true Japanese way, but our focus today is in finding your reason. In the West, the concept of Ikigai is represented in the form of a Venn diagram with four sets of overlapping circles. Every circle represents a category.

Today's exercise will require creating this diagram and working towards finding your Ikigai.

For each category, use the prompts below to reflect:

- **What do you love doing?**
  - What activities did you do in the past that brought you joy and happiness?
  - What activities do you currently enjoy doing?
- **What are you good at?**
  - What are your strengths?
  - What do people usually ask you for help with?
- **What does the world need?**
  - What inspires you in the world?
  - Who are the people who inspire you and why?
  - What issues in the world move you?
- **What can you get paid for?**
  - What services or products could you sell?
  - What job could you do?

Once you're done, fill in the diagram with your answers. Next, look for connections between each of the circles. For example, what are you good at that the world needs? What do you love doing that you can also get paid for? Establishing these connections will help you find the perfect balance between your passion, mission, profession and vocation. Armed with that information, you can now make better decisions on things in which you can get involved in to live your purpose.

CHAPTER 25

Just Listen

———

"When you talk, you are only repeating what you already

know. But if you listen, you may learn something new."

—DALAI LAMA

How good of a listener are you?

If you were to rate your listening skill on a scale of 1 to 10, how much would you give yourself? Do you pay attention when people talk to you, or do you tend to be distracted? Research estimates that in average, we only remember between 25 and 50 percent of what we hear. As shocking as this statistic sounds, it's not surprising as we often overestimate our abilities. We believe that we are listening, but only a few of us do so effectively. In a world dominated by bite-sized tweets and visual storytelling, genuinely listening to each other has become increasingly difficult. We're more connected than ever and yet we are further disconnected. Our attention span has crumbled tragically and proper communication is nowhere to be found. With all the noise and the distraction, what we deem as listening is actually just hearing, but there is a difference between them.

HEARING VS. LISTENING

Meet Erika and Diana.

In a conversation, Erika is the type that will barely let you finish a sentence. It even feels like a monologue at times. It's not so much about what one has to say but what matters to her. She might even change the subject if it's of no interest to her or rashly brush it off. If you try to put a word in, she won't allow you to finish your train of thought before trying to place a comment. And besides, while she is talking to you, she is likely fidgeting with her phone.

Then there's Diana. Diana is the type that won't interject and interrupt the flow of the conversation and will, instead, allow it to take its course. She is tuned in and exhibits how interested she is in your thoughts and ideas—she doesn't drift away. Physically and verbally, you can tell that she is present.

So, are you more like Erika or Diana? See if any of these apply to you:

- You want to direct the flow of the conversation by offering up ideas.

- You're impatient and your body language shows to the speaker that you're not interested.

- You think of the answer or the solution before the other person is done talking.

- You like to multitask when listening to people.

Most of us would like to think that we are more like Diana than Erika. If we are honest with ourselves, we may see that we exhibit Erika's tendencies more often than Diana's. The difference between Diana and Erika can be summed up like this: Erika was hearing, but Diana was listening.

Understanding the difference between hearing and listening is critical for a successful life. Hearing is your brain's automatic response to sound. It's effortless and purely accidental. We hear sounds all the time, and we filter them as they come, deciding on what matters and what doesn't. Meanwhile, listening is meaningful and focused.

THE ART OF ACTIVE LISTENING

Listening is a skill and can therefore be improved. We all want to be seen, so why shouldn't we make the effort to try and see others? The best way to truly do this is to listen actively when they speak. Whether we agree or disagree with what a person may be saying, it's a sign of respect and commitment when you listen to someone. You may be born with the gift of hearing, but active listening is something you nurture and develop.

Active listening is one that requires that we thoroughly absorb, understand and respond to what is being said. It's being attentive to verbal and non-verbal forms of communication. As Peter Drucker said, "The most important thing in communication is hearing what isn't said." By improving your active listening skills, you'll add many benefits to your life, like:

Deeper connections and relationships

By listening actively, people are likely to open up more and build better rapport with you. They will view you as someone they can rely on and will respond better to you.

More understanding

Conflicts and disagreements are bound to happen in the course of your life. When a person feels as if their concerns are being listened to, the chances for understanding and resolution will be higher, and harmony will exist.

Improved confidence

By being intentional with your listening, you'll have healthier and more robust conversations in your life. This will create a positive feedback loop, which will eventually boost your self-esteem and confidence.

ACTIVE LISTENING

Keeping the above in mind, you'll start to find yourself talking less and listening more. As a result, you'll become less likely to miss critical information. This also means that you'll be more attuned to locate new opportunities and act on essential things. Statistics show that less than 2% of all professionals have had training on listening skills. With practice, you can start improving your active listening skills. So, how can you improve them?

Consider the following tips for a start:

IN ACTION: ACTIVE LISTENING	
Instead of:	**Consider this:**
Asking close-ended questions.	**Ask open-ended questions**. This will encourage the other person to keep talking.
Being distracted.	**Remove distractions** that could block you from actively listening.
Ignoring your body language.	**Mirror the posture** of the person speaking and maintain eye contact.
Playing the guessing game	**Take a self-assessment test** online or offline.
Rushing the pace of the conversation.	**Paraphrase and summarize what you are hearing**. This will also help clarify the communication so there's no misunderstanding.
Trying to fill every gap in a conversation with words.	**Enjoy taking pauses** and get comfortable with silence.

BETTER TIP

With

JULIAN TREASURE

A sought-after communication expert, Julian Treasure has dedicated the last twenty years to developing business and personal communication in sound. His TED Talk, "5 ways to listen better", is one of the most watched of all time. From that talk, here are his five strategies to improve your listening skills:

1. **Silence:** embracing silence for just three minutes a day will help reset your ears. We are so used to noise that we no longer value silence.

2. **The mixer:** wherever you find yourself, at any given moment, try to tune in and absorb every sound. Try to identify the different channels of noise around you. This helps improve the quality of your listening.

3. **Savoring:** start enjoying the mundane sounds—the whirring of the coffee machine, the loud hair dryer blows and the microwave buzzes. The idea is that mundane sounds are the "hidden choir". You'll only notice it if you pay attention. So do so.

4. **Listening positions:** your listening positions matter. Every situation is different so adapt your positions to what's appropriate: active vs. passive, critical or sympathetic etc.

5. **RASA:** an acronym to use while communicating. It stands for Receive, Appreciate, Summary and Ask.

    -   **R**eceive by paying attention to the person

    -   **A**ppreciate by making verbal noises to acknowledge you are present

    -   **S**ummarize by using words like "so"

    -   **A**sk by asking questions afterwards

Keep this in mind during your next conversation!

A BETTER YOU

In Action

ASKING OPEN-ENDED QUESTIONS

Ever had a conversation and you felt there wasn't a connection? There is a chance that you were asking close-ended questions instead of open-ended ones. The difference? A close-ended question is one in which the person usually answers with one word: a "yes" or a "no". On the other hand, an open ended-question encourages and moves people to keep the conversation going.

Close-ended question	Open-ended question
Have you been anxious?	How have you been feeling lately?
Do you need a new job?	What change do you need?

How can you ask more open-ended questions?

- Ask questions that follow "what", "when", "who", "where" and "why" (know when to use why)

For today's exercise, I want you to commit to asking one person you see or meet more open-ended questions. Here are some prompts using the "W's" to get you started (note that you should adapt as necessary to your conversations):

- What do you think ... ?
- How did you ... ?
- How might you ... ?
- Who do you think ... ?
- When should we ... ?

CHAPTER 26

You, Inc.

—

"We are all salesmen every day of our lives. We are selling our ideas, our plans, our enthusiasms to those with whom we come in contact."

—CHARLES R. SCHWAB

E dwige, your phone is ringing!"
My father was shouting his lungs out from the basement, waiting
for my mother to pick up her phone. We could all hear her infamous
ringtone and I was pretty sure she could hear it too. But we also knew
that there was a higher chance for it to snow during the summer than
for my mother to pick up her noisy phone. My mother purposefully
assigned a similar ringtone for all her saved contacts, so anytime the
phone rang differently she flat-out refused to pick up the call.

My mother was adamant that the only people calling her from an
unknown number were "sleazy salespeople", and she wanted nothing
to do with them. For someone who enjoyed shopping so much, I've
always been surprised by her level of discomfort and mistrust of them.
But, as I later found out, my mother was far from being the only one
who disliked their kind. An annual Gallup poll surveyed Americans
and asked them to rate twenty careers for their honesty and ethics. The
survey's findings indicate that out of the top five worst professions, at
least four were sales related: stockbrokers, telemarketers, advertising
practitioners and car salespersons. No wonder then that the word
"sales" had such a negative connotation.

The more I dug and tried to understand the sales profession's bad
rap, the more I heard of stories of deceit, manipulation and pushy tactics.
Like in every career, I believe poor behavior from a few bad apples has
given the entire profession a bad name, when in reality there are honest
and caring sales professionals who uphold the highest standards. When
we talk about sales, we tend to forget one important fact—we are all
salespeople. You are sold to, but you are also selling. And if you want to

get everything you want, both personally and professionally, there is no running away from selling in your day-to-day life. If you think you're not selling, think again!

YOU ARE ALWAYS SELLING

Yes, you are. Every day of your life. No matter where you live. No matter your occupation, you are selling. Just because you're not trying to sell a product or a service, doesn't mean you're not in the sales business. Being a salesperson doesn't require a uniform or a title. Every day you sell dreams, stories and experiences. Think about it. Whenever you're trying to sway people towards your point of view, talking during an interview, pitching a new idea at work or to a client, enticing your kids to behave the right way, convincing your boss to give you a promotion or getting investors to buy into your company—you are in the business of selling. You are selling your ideas, your skills, your credentials, your personality. And if you don't accept this fact, you'll keep wondering why things are not working out for you. I believe that thriving personally and professionally is proportional to the degree at which you sell your story, your vision and your value better than the person next to you.

SELLING IS PERSUADING

Selling is essentially persuading someone else to do something for you. Your success in life largely rests on your ability to convince others to collaborate with you and to give you what you desire. The problem is that most of us have a hard time persuading people. Do any of these statements sound familiar?

- You don't know how to communicate your ideas and what you have to offer.

- You can't get the support and resources you need to create progress in your life.

- You don't feel like you're seen and heard.

- You believe you're often overlooked for positions you deserve and qualify for.

It's impossible to run away from persuading people around us because we have to do it every day. But, if it's that important, why the lack of emphasis on selling skills? Why don't we embrace it more and hate it less? Perhaps because of our aversion to the word "sales" or simply misunderstanding the reality that we are always selling something. In any case, the good things in life belong to those who are convincing and sell the best.

THE ART OF PERSUASION

To live is to persuade. As Tony Robbins puts it, "Power today is the ability to communicate and the ability to persuade. If you're a persuader with no legs, you'll persuade someone to carry you. If you have no money, you'll persuade someone to lend you some. Persuasion may be the ultimate skill for creating change." It would be wise for us to shift our mindset. We spend our lives communicating and interacting with others, and since we don't inhabit deserted islands, we need to collaborate and entice other people to achieve what we want. Shunning the idea of selling and persuading won't help us in any way. This mindset is not about having a big ego or manipulating people to accept your ideas, vision or advice. On the contrary, it's about caring about what other people want and becoming better at promoting what you have to offer to ultimately get the quality of life you desire.

To improve your persuasion abilities, consider the following ideas to get you started:

IN ACTION: PERSUADING BETTER	
Instead of:	**Consider this:**
Trying to persuade someone who is not interested.	**Aim to build rapport first** so that people can be more comfortable with you.
Trying to convince someone by being forceful.	**Use the "But You're Free" (BYAF)** technique. When you make a request, add at the end: *"But you are free to do so."* This reaffirms the person's free will and because of that, they are more likely to say "yes". Weird? Sure, but it works.
Directly making a small request or asking for a small favor.	**Try the "Door-in-the-Face" technique.** Start by making a huge request first. It's likely that they will say "no" to your big request. Go back and make a smaller request (the one you desired all along). It's likely they will find that one more reasonable and say "yes".
Directly making a big request or asking for a big favor.	**Give the "Foot-in-the-door" technique a go** if you need to ask for a big favor. How it works? You start by asking a small favor first. By doing so, you're getting the other person involved and committed to helping you. By asking for a small favor, you're increasing your chances to go for the big ask.

BETTER TIP

With

DR. ROBERT CIALDINI

Dr. Robert Cialdini, a psychology expert and marketing genius, has researched and identified six core principles that can help anyone become more persuasive and move people to change behaviors. So what are they?

1. **Reciprocity:** this principle is based on the fact that people like to return favors. In practice, make sure you do right by people and they will do right by you.

2. **Commitment and consistency:** once people make a small commitment, they will likely remain consistent and be willing to do and give more. In practice, this is about asking people to make small, insignificant commitments at first, which will then pave the way for bigger requests.

3. **Social proof:** we humans like to fit in. Because of this, we look out to others and see how we should behave, think and do things. In practice, if you want someone to take an action, connect with that person's peers or even more influential people who have already taken the same action.

4. **Liking:** people tend to be easily convinced by individuals they like. In practice, this means that you need to find common ground with people before trying to persuade them.

5. **Authority:** people are more likely to follow you if they perceive you as an expert. This means establishing and showing your authority through your degrees, accolades, experience and other aspects that signal authority.

6. **Scarcity:** admit it. You like exclusivity and things that aren't widely accessible. To be successful at this, always aim to convey a sense of urgency when you're trying to convince others.

A BETTER YOU

In Action

PRACTICING PERSUASION TECHNIQUES

There are various ways to convince others, and we've touched on a few of them already. For today's exercise, I want you to try at least one. You're going to be the one to decide the "when" and the "who", but you must commit to trying one today with at least three people. Think about where your life is right now and what method you think will be most valuable to you in this moment. Here's a reminder of the techniques:

- **But You Are Free (BYAF):** when you make a request, add at the end: "But you are free to do so".

- **Door-in-the-Face:** this is about making a huge request first. If they say no, you go back and make a small request.

- **Foot-in-the-door:** best used if you need to ask for a big favor but you don't want to scare people away. How does it work? You start by asking a small favor first. Then after getting that teeny tiny favor, you'll proceed to a slightly bigger favor. Continuing that ladder to land on the biggest favor.

Once you've finished the task (applying the techniques on three different people), I want you to reflect on your experience:

- How did you feel?

- What was the outcome?

- How do you think you could do things differently?

- What else was missing?

Practice makes perfect. Journal each of your experiences and reflect what you could've done better. Rinse and repeat until you get it just right!

CHAPTER 27

Promote Yourself

—

"You have to be the one promoting yourself. If you don't think that you're worthy, you're never going to make it."

—MISTY COPELAND

Ever heard the saying: "If you build it, they will come?" The iconic quote, a variation of a line from the 1989 movie *Field of Dreams* is widely referenced in popular culture. The quote seems to imply that if you have an idea, a product or a service, all you have to do is to launch it and customers will magically clamor to you. How often do you buy products and services that you've never heard of? Build it and they will come is a myth and a trap that many entrepreneurs have fallen for. Sometimes entrepreneurs get so caught up on product development, always adding bells and whistles, that they blindly believe that customers will just come and sweep all their stock up from the shelves. I too have been there. As ill-fated as that approach is, many of us have adopted it in our lives, especially in our professional ones.

How many times have you heard that all you need to do is to get good grades, put your head down, work hard, get more qualifications and just produce quality results to get rewarded and recognized for your efforts? Well, how is that working out for you? I know how that went for me. I did work hard. I did put my head down. I got the additional qualifications. And every time I did, it seemed as if it was never enough. I kept wondering what I was missing? I thought they said get more and you'll be more. Why wasn't the "more" finally unlocking the doors and getting me a seat at the table(s) I so desired? What could I have been doing wrong? Well, I was doing everything except that I wasn't promoting myself! As Toba Beta put it, "While you are so busy trying to make yourself humble, many are persistently and quietly promoting themselves." And, just as many entrepreneurs neglect the promotional aspect in their business plan and miraculously expect customers to flock to them, this is also how we neglect promoting ourselves.

OUR RELATIONSHIP WITH SELF-PROMOTION

Self-promotion is a phrase that makes us cringe. The Macmillan dictionary defines self-promotion as "Attempts to make people notice you." If that doesn't sound negative enough, here are some synonyms of the word: showing off, boastful, attention seeking, bragging, self-congratulatory. It's no surprise then that we shy away from being seen as self-promoters! And then we also have various societal norms that make it hard for us to talk freely about our accomplishments:

Perceptions

The fear of being seen as narcissistic. We don't want to be seen as arrogant or "full of ourselves". This holds us back from tooting our own horns.

Upbringing

Sometimes the culture and society we were raised in may have shunned our outward expression. Expressions such as "don't draw attention to yourself" and "don't contradict people" may very well have been part of the vocabulary you heard growing up. We then become afraid to show up as our full authentic self.

Bias and gender differences

Studies indicate that women experience backlash when they self-promote because of ingrained traditional gender roles through which women are supposed to be passive and subservient. On the other hand, men are encouraged to be bold, to push the envelope, ask questions and demand what they deserve.

Imposter syndrome

Imposter syndrome is chronic self-doubt and a belief that we aren't as qualified as others see us. When we suffer from imposter syndrome, we feel like a fraud and will tend to attribute our accomplishments to sheer luck.

So, because of all these factors, as well as others not listed here, many of us are fearful of self-promotion. So what do we end up doing instead? We wait. Like a planet in a foreign galaxy, we wait to be discovered, to be given the opportunity to share our ideas and to advocate for ourselves. Are you waiting to be discovered? Do any of these sound familiar to you?

- You underplay your achievements.

- You don't like to take credit for your work because you think the recognition should always be attributed to the entire team.

- You believe that great work always speaks for itself and you shouldn't have to "show off".

- You are hoping people will notice your achievements.

- You have trouble speaking about your skills and talents.

- You don't want to talk about your accomplishments for fear of appearing boastful.

If you find yourself nodding to any of these statements, don't stress. You're not the only one.

SELF-PROMOTION IS SELF-ADVOCACY

Speaking up for and about yourself is a critical life skill that needs to be developed. But due to some of the reasons I highlighted earlier, most of us fear self-promotion. But it doesn't have to be the scary monster we picture it to be. A different way of seeing things might help.

I grew up wary of the phrase "self-promotion" but with time I have redefined it for myself and decided to embrace the term "self-advocacy". Self-advocacy is not about being a show off, beating your chest and shouting about all that you have accomplished. Self-advocacy is about championing your needs and having the confidence to share your accomplishments, skills and abilities. Self-advocacy is a significant asset on your path to success, enabling you to communicate your impact and value to others in an effective and meaningful way.

I used to be a member of what author Meredith Fineman dubbed the "Qualified Quiet": smart people who show up, get the work done but don't know how to showcase their accomplishments. In many ways, I was like those entrepreneurs who were always developing products but failed to promote them. I thought that since I was talented, well-educated and a champion at getting things done, it was enough for me to get noticed, appreciated and promoted in my professional life. But, as I unfortunately found out, this type of mindset barely ever takes you places. In fact, thinking like this will make you miss opportunities and could lead to resentment and unhappiness. It's a realization that I came to late, but as they say, "better now than never".

On the other hand, I witnessed how my friend Maggy's career soared. She knew how to speak about herself. She was audacious and unapologetic about the abilities, skills and the value she had to offer. Did she have all the answers? No. Did she wait to get all the qualifications they kept telling her she needed? No. Did she let her work speak for itself? Yes. She delivered quality work but she also spoke up about the person behind that work—herself. And that made a significant difference. Now she's thriving and moving up the ladder in her professional life, breaking glass ceilings in the process. If I learned anything from people like Maggy, it's that relying on your work ethic, achievements and abilities is simply not enough. Self-advocacy is not arrogant. On the contrary, it's transformative.

ADVOCATING BETTER FOR YOURSELF

Advocating for yourself requires a change in perspective. Self-advocacy is about storytelling, reframing the stories you tell yourself and the ones you tell others.

For yourself

It starts with a mindset shift. Start by seeing self-advocacy as giving instead of taking. Think about it. The sum of all your accomplishments, abilities, ideas and gifts are valuable to others. By sharing what you are capable of doing, you could be changing lives and maybe even the world. People aren't mind readers. If people can't find you or don't know that you exist, well then how on earth are they supposed to know what you are capable of doing! Every one of us wants to connect with talented, knowledgeable people who can bring value to our lives. And if you are that person, you need to make it easier for people to notice and find you.

For others

People like stories. Individually and collectively, we enjoy hearing stories and we enjoy telling them. We especially like stories in which we can play a part. I firmly believe that people are genuinely good and would always want to contribute to your success if given the opportunity. Advocating for yourself is about telling your most authentic story—stories about your path, accomplishments, goals and what you are up to. By backing up your stories with facts and the results you have achieved, you will turn mere strangers into ambassadors who will further advocate for you and spread the word about you even when you are not in the room.

Advocating for yourself is a lifelong commitment, it's not something that you do part-time. You don't just turn on the switch for self-advocacy when you are asked to give a speech or when you are sitting at a performance review. If you want to get further in life and realize your dreams, you have to make it a daily habit. By making it a part of your day-to-day lifestyle, it will become much easier for you to speak about your accomplishments. But how do you do it? Here are some ideas to make self-promotion/self-advocacy (whatever you decide to call it!) a constant part of your life.

IN ACTION: SELF-PROMOTION	
Instead of:	**Consider this:**
Demonstrating a lack of confidence.	**Know yourself.** Be aware of your abilities, strengths and your goals. Know what you have to offer and know what you want. Revisit chapter two if needed.
Letting people tell your story for you.	**Hone your storytelling skills and craft a compelling narrative about yourself.** You know what you want and know what you have to offer. Now craft a story you would want to share. This is not just about restating your resume.
Thinking you have nothing valuable to offer.	**Improve your confidence.** Work on changing your mindset and eradicate limiting beliefs. Revisit the chapter on believing in yourself if needed.
Going at it alone without support.	**Build your network.** Invest time and energy in nurturing the relationships you have and build new ones.

BETTER TIP

With

PEGGY KLAUS

When it comes down to the art of promotion, look no further than communication coach and author, Peggy Klaus. Claus has a list of twelve tips to keep in mind as you embrace self-promotion.

Here they are:

1. Be your best authentic self.
2. Think about to whom you are tooting.
3. Say it with meaningful and entertaining stories.
4. Keep it short and simple.
5. Talk with them, not at them.
6. Be able to back up what you say.
7. Know when to self-promote.
8. Turn small talk into big talk.
9. Keep your bragging rights current and fresh.
10. Be ready at a moment's notice.
11. Have a sense of humor.
12. Use all your senses to connect better: your eyes, ears, head and heart.

A BETTER YOU

In Action

CRAFTING YOUR ELEVATOR PITCH

Imagine that you find yourself in an elevator, at an event or in a room with someone you always wanted to impress, work for or do business with. What would you say? How would you describe yourself? What will your message be?

As the great philosopher Seneca said, "Luck is what happens when preparation meets opportunity." So, there's no time to be tripping over words when you finally get the opportunity to connect with new people. You need to be prepared and have an elevator pitch. That is, a short descriptive sentence or two that sums up who you are and what you are all about.

Remember to keep it concise, say between 30-60 seconds maximum. Your elevator pitch is not the time to tell your whole life story, so keep it short and snappy. It just needs to give enough essential info while also sparking the listener's curiosity so that they want to know more about you. But how do you go about creating it? Craft your pitch around these three key points:

- **The basics about you:** who you are, what you do and where you work (if that applies).

- **The value you bring:** what sets you apart. What have you learned. Mention your strengths and skills.

- **Your interests:** what do you want to achieve and what are you interested in.

Before you can develop your elevator pitch, you need to know your goals and strengths. If you've skipped the chapters on these subjects, I suggest you revisit them. Next time someone asks you "Tell me more about yourself", you will be prepared!

It's important that you don't use industry jargon that makes it difficult to understand. Also make sure that you adapt your elevator pitch as much as possible to your audience.

Having said all that, it's time to dive in! For today's exercise, you will spend time crafting your elevator pitch. Follow the prompts above and write it all down in your own notebook/journal. Again, practice makes perfect. It's imperative that you practice saying your elevator pitch frequently.

CHAPTER 28

Your Network Is Your Net Worth

—

"The richest people in the world look for and build

networks. Everyone else looks for work."

—ROBERT KIYOSAKI

Networking. When you think of it, do you picture an event with a sea of people sharing business cards, trying to rack up as many numbers as possible?

For a lot of people, this is exactly how they were first introduced to the practice. Over time, we've come to view these events as the totality of networking. We've also become accustomed to seeing networking as a selfish activity, a "give me, give me" activity that we should only engage in when we're looking to push a business or when we're trying to find a job. But what if we had it wrong? What if instead of thinking of networking as another chore on our ever-expanding to-do lists, we embrace it as a way of life?

THE POWER OF NETWORKING

Our lives are a web of networks. As I see it, networking is simply the exchange of information and ideas among people within our professional and social circles. The standard definition of a network is a "group or system of interconnected people or things." No matter who you are and where you live, you have an existing network: former classmates, friends, family, clients, colleagues—all these people make up your network. We rely on our existing networks for advice on where to shop, who to date, what to study and for a myriad other things in our day-to-day lives. Think about the last time you wanted to make an important decision, what did you do? I bet you reached out to your network to pool and sort out the information before taking further steps.

But not all networks are the same. Just like there's a difference in connection speed between 2G, 3G and 5G networks, your personal and professional networks also differ. The strength of our connections impact all aspects of our lives but few of us realize this. It's a shame that so many people don't fully invest in nurturing, strengthening and growing their networks. Does this sound like you?

- You think about networking only when you need a new work opportunity.
- You don't nurture your current network.
- You don't follow up when you meet new people.
- You think you only need to connect with influential, powerful people.
- You think that only extroverts have the capacity to network and that doesn't apply to you.

The old adage, "It's not what you know, it's who you know" neatly sums up the importance of having a strong network. Want to progress and achieve your goals? You simply can't do it alone. Life is a big network of connections, and thinking that you can realize your ambitions without collaborating with others is foolhardy.

THE BENEFITS OF A NETWORK

There exists an African proverb, "If you want to go quickly, go alone. If you want to go far, go together." It's no accident that those who have achieved incredible success have more often than not done so with the support of other people. On your path to success you'll also need to work, collaborate and be supported by many people, and that's not a bad thing! That's what networking is about—building relationships. Taking the time to build and nurture these relationships has significant lifelong benefits:

Increased access

What's the difference between knowing or not knowing? Access. There are countless things happening around you all the time and you can't be everywhere all at once. But some people in your network might. Think of your network as an extension of who you are.

Access leads to opportunities

You'll be able to have access to expertise and resources to help you move forward. You could have all the talent and qualifications in the world and still struggle to get to where you want to be. It's said that around 80% of all jobs are acquired through relationships, so your network could be the bridge between you and the perfect career or business opportunity. If you don't have a solid network, you could very likely end up in the cold.

Opportunities lead to visibility

The more opportunities you get, the more visible you'll be. This means that you'll be able to showcase your talents and skills to a wider audience. If you want to be on people's radars, build your network. You just can't afford to leave it to luck alone.

Something to keep in mind though: building your network is not a competition. It's the quality of your relationships that counts, not the quantity.

BUILDING YOUR NETWORK

Networking is not a once-off deal, it is a way of life.

Networking should be an everyday thing. You are networking when you chit-chat with your neighbors, when you talk to a fellow passenger on a train ride or when you form a connection with the person in front of you in the queue at your regular coffee shop.

Networking happens in the small moments.
Small moments lead to big breakthroughs

So, what can you do to build, nurture and strengthen your network?

Change your mindset

Build your network on a daily basis. Remember, it's a journey not a destination. It's not something you do only when you feel like it or when you are invited to an event. Every moment of your life presents an opportunity for you to network. The most important connections in your life happen in less formal moments: using public transport, taking a group workout class or even mowing your lawn.

Be curious

Stop thinking that you only need to connect with people who have already made it, you know, the rich, famous and influential. There's no doubt that influential people are inspiring. You can learn a lot from them. But you can learn from everyone around you. Each person has a story and a network. They don't have to be on the cover of Time or Forbes magazine to warrant a connection. Start by being genuinely interested in who they are, what they do and what makes them tick.

Give more than you take

Networking is pouring into others as much as you want them to invest in you—building and nurturing authentic relationships with people based on shared interests and goals. Think more about what you can do for others first. Every time you help someone you are building trust, and this can turn a simple connection into a friendship. And friends help friends.

Here are some more ways you can develop your network:

IN ACTION: BUILDING YOUR NETWORK

Instead of:	Consider this:
Waiting for things to just happen.	**Be strategic.** While you can network every day and everywhere, having a plan helps!
Leaving it to chance.	**Decide which online/offline activities** you like and want to engage in, and which contacts you need to follow up on.
Faking it	**Be yourself.** Choose networking activities that complement your personality. You'll make a good impression in places where you can be yourself.
Not keeping in touch.	**Follow up.** Connecting with people is one thing. You can only truly build relationships and trust if you stay in touch with people.

BETTER TIP

With

KEITH FERRAZZI

Author and speaker Keith Ferrazzi is well regarded as an expert on relationship building. There is no better "go-to" person for tips on the networking front.

- ✓ **Build it before you need it:** you don't wake up one day and have a network. You have to invest in it and build it gradually before you ever need it.

- ✓ **Develop a networking action plan:** if you know the goals you want to accomplish, you have to connect these goals with people, places and things to help you make it happen. Find the people who can help you reach these goals, and have an action plan on how you will connect with them.

- ✓ **Be generous:** help others without wanting anything in return. Be invested in other people's success first.

- ✓ **Be organized:** many people think they don't know anyone or don't have anyone in their network.

- ✓ **Be genuine:** truly connect with people and don't just focus on what you want to get out of them. Build genuine relationships based on mutual interests.

- ✓ **Do your homework:** before you reach out and meet people, take the time to find out more about them.

- ✓ **Do ask for help:** don't be afraid to ask for help when it comes to introductions. If you don't ask, you won't get it.

- ✓ **Do follow up:** reach out to people in your network frequently, not just when you need something from them. Maintaining the connection is just as important as establishing it.

A BETTER YOU

In Action

YOUR NETWORKING ACTION PLAN

For today's exercise we are focusing on developing your networking action plan. Start by:

- **Defining your goals for the next 12-24 months.** I suggest you define your professional and personal goals differently. Keep the chapter on goals on hand when you do so.

- **Knowing who to add to your network.** Given your goals, who are the people you need in your network to help you achieve them? If you already have links to the people you need:

o Write their names down.

o Work out what the one thing is that you need to do to engage more with these people. Reach out to them by email or connect in-person or virtually, and offer to help them out on something they need.

o Whatever you decide, write it down and commit a deadline to it.

If you don't have the right people in your network:

- Assess if anyone in your existing network may be able to help with connecting you.

- Figure out what the one thing is that you need to do to engage more with these people. Email them or set up a meeting.

- Make sure that you write it down and set a deadline to keep you on track.

Be sure to tell someone about your networking plan so that they can hold you accountable and follow your progress.

CHAPTER 29

You 2.0

—

"Your life can end at any time, and it can end more than once. But it can also begin more than once."

—MICHAEL R. FRENCH

D o you believe in reincarnation?" asked Marcia.

"What?" I replied, stunned.

"Yes, reincarnation," exclaimed Marcia, looking at me curiously. "Do you think when we die, we'll keep coming back to another body to live more lives?"

"Huh?" I paused. "Very deep. You woke up philosophical today, huh?" I asked as I kept looking through the menu. "I have never met anyone who was reincarnated. So dolly, I don't know."

"Hmm, true," she said softly. "Don't you find the thought at least comforting though?"

"Comforting? What could be comforting about it?" I asked.

"Thinking that if you fail to do it right in this life, you can have a do-over and make things right in another life," she responded, looking up and then away.

"Another life!" I snorted. "Count me out of your next life's plans," I replied, rather mockingly.

"I'm being serious," she insisted.

"Okay!" I said. "We have this one life. One! But it doesn't mean that we have to live it only one way. We can live in so many different chapters."

"And, you know what?" I asked as I reached out for her hands. "The beauty of life is that we can always change direction. We get the chance to change, grow and evolve time and time again."

TO LIVE IS TO EVOLVE

At times, professionally and personally, we feel like we're on hamster wheel and just can't get off it. We are restless and no longer satisfied with where we are. As Heraclitus said, change is the only constant thing in life. Life is about cycles, and with all the rapid changes happening around us, we need to be able to adapt, grow and evolve if we want to reach our full potential. But with our hamster wheels spinning around so fast, it can be easy not to recognize when it's time for change. Do you identify with any of these statements?

- You find that you really need to pump yourself up to do anything.
- You often catch yourself daydreaming.
- You are envious of others and wish you were them.
- You feel unfulfilled and disconnected from your goals and dreams.
- You get excited at the thought of doing something completely different.

If this resonates with you, it might be time to reinvent yourself.

THE NEED FOR SELF-REINVENTION

To reinvent oneself is to "produce something new that is based on something that already exists." The concept of reinvention sounds terrifying and wrongly assumes that it requires a complete overhaul: throwing out who we are, all that we have done and adopting a new personality and starting all over again. But it doesn't have to be so drastic and dramatic. I like to compare the concept of reinvention to computer software that needs to be regularly updated. In this process, the existing software on the device is not replaced, it's merely fine-tuned by removing outdated features. Ultimately, the updates are meant to make the software perform more reliably and faster.

Reinventing yourself goes beyond the superficial aspects of your life. You know, the part everyone sees: the hair, the weight, the outfits, etc. It doesn't stop at changing your looks, moving to a new place, switching jobs and appearing different. If anything, self-reinvention is more about staying true to who you really are. It's about total alignment with your values and using your past experiences as stepping stones to evolve into the best version of yourself. You are reinventing yourself when you decide to change your old ways and forge a new path by exploring novel opportunities and possibilities. You know you're ready for self-reinvention when you feel:

Disconnected from your goals

Sometimes instead of living, we let life pass us by. One day we wake up and realize we're far from where we're meant to be. If you feel like your life has taken a detour, it's time to bring it into alignment.

Uninspired and listless

You don't feel any joy in what you're doing and you imagine yourself being somewhere else, doing something different. You're probably also burnt out from taking on so much, with your mental and physical well-being out of sync.

A lack of growth

Growth is an essential part of our learning and development. If you feel bored, stuck and no longer excited about the path you're on, then it's time to take yourself out of your comfort zone.

THE PATH TO SELF-REINVENTION

Life may throw circumstances at you that push you towards reinvention. Or you may have simply decided that you need to get off your hamster wheel and initiate the transformation yourself. I've had to reinvent myself a couple of times already, and what really made the difference was taking small steps to create a shift forward. This ultimately brought my dreams and goals into alignment. Your circumstances will be different, of course, and you may have no choice but to take drastic decisions to create fulfillment and purpose in your life.

Whatever the case, know that there's no right or perfect way to go about reinventing yourself. As much as we want instant solutions to our problems, reinventing oneself is not an overnight solution. You might be tempted to take drastic steps and rush towards making life-changing decisions. But once the adrenaline fueled by your desire for change wears off, you'll be back at your starting point. Self-reinvention requires small, consistent steps. That's where you'll be able to attain sustainable progress.

While self-reinvention can be daunting, here are a few pointers to help you get started on this journey.

IN ACTION: REINVENTING YOURSELF	
Instead of:	**Consider this:**
Rushing to get started.	**Observe and introspect**. Don't rush things. This is the time for introspection and self-awareness. You have to know why you desire to reinvent yourself. What is it that you need to change?
Being stuck with what you know.	**Embrace learning.** Some habits are keeping you from living the life you are meant to live. Start building new habits and acquiring new skills.
Living a life you don't want.	**Listen to yourself.** Know your vision. Where are you now and where do you want to be? See the chapter on finding your why.
Running toward change blindly.	**Build a plan of action**. Turn your vision into goals. See the chapter on goals to help you develop smart goals.

BETTER STORY

With

AVA DUVERNAY

How can you make a career switch from one industry to the next and dominate it? Is it possible to go from publicist to a world renowned director and producer? If "anything is possible" were a person, it would be Ava Duvernay.

Ava Duvernay's bold reinvention from marketing and public relations expert to major movie director has been far from traditional. While Ava had always been in the movie industry as a publicist, she didn't study at film school. In fact, she only started working behind a camera at the age of 32 and only made her first movie by age 35. In a world that is bent on telling us to rush everything, she is a reminder that one can start and re-start at any time if you have the passion, courage and grit to do so. For over a decade Ava excelled at PR and even created her own agency to help promote other people's movies. And while it was clear that she had a passion for the film industry, she had no formal training in filmmaking. But she embarked on the transition from publicist to filmmaker at her own pace, gradually but strategically.

Duvernay did it all by banking on herself: she followed her passion and invested her own money in producing her first three movies, all while still holding down her job as a publicist. Her path clearly shows that it's never too late to change course, and that success happens when you take baby steps. Taking focused steps has helped cement Ava Duvernay's reputation as one of the most influential and respected film directors in the industry today. And if she could do it, there's no reason why you can't either!

A BETTER YOU

In Action

THE REINVENTION WHEEL

Reinventing yourself is not all black and white. Finding out if you need professional or personal reinvention will come from a combination of things. But you can't reinvent what you don't know. By now, you have built self-awareness and you have defined what it is that you want to accomplish. If you haven't, I recommend you do so by revisiting the chapters on goals and defining your vision first.

For today's exercise, we are going to build on a concept called the six dimensions of wellness model which was developed by Dr. Bill Helter.

- There are six categories in the wheel: emotional, physical, intellectual, spiritual, social, and occupational (work, career, etc.).

- For each category, write down one thing that you currently enjoy doing and one thing you would like to start doing.

NEXT STEPS:

- If there's nothing positive you could write in a particular category, this is a red flag. It either means you have not invested enough in that category in your everyday life or whatever you are doing is not bringing you any joy, peace and happiness.

- For all the things you want to start doing: try to see if there's a pattern in what you have written down. Decide and put a deadline to how you can start doing more of these things.

CHAPTER 30

The Art Of Gratitude

—

"The soul that gives thanks can find comfort in everything;

the soul that complains can find comfort in nothing"

—HANNAH WHITALL SMITH

How often do you complain? Once a day? Twice? Too often? Oh well, like so many of us, I bet you don't keep count. Complaining flows so easily out of our mouths that we barely notice when we do it. Complaining is often used to describe a variety of behaviors, but as I see it, we engage in the art of complaining when we vent and dwell on things that are out of our control. Research indicates that the average person complains about once a minute in every discussion. As absurd as that may sound, if you need any further proof of how commonplace complaining has become, spend some time on social media.

Complaining can be so comforting too. Truth be told, it's easy to find endless things to moan about—from the weather that messed up our mood, to the co-worker who always "steals" our lunch. The list is endless. And while complaining is not the same as just stating your needs and expressing your emotions, it can be easy to confuse the two. The occasional venting session may seem harmless at first, but before long it creeps in and solidifies its place as a habit. In fact, we've become such habitual complainers that some of us use it as a bonding tool. You may not want to admit it, but if you pay close attention there are people in your circle with whom you formed a bond around a common joy for complaining. Scary. But every time we complain we are essentially taking responsibility off ourselves and jumping into victim mode. Unfortunately, the more we complain, the less we see the beauty and the possibilities which surround us. And just as there will always be something to complain about, there is also always going to be something to be grateful for.

THE POWER OF GRATITUDE

What is gratitude? To be grateful is simply to give thanks—to have a thankful appreciation for what we have, either tangible or intangible. At any given moment in our lives, we are faced with situations and events outside of our control. And while we're unable to control these events, by cultivating an attitude of gratitude we can help shift our perspective and our reactions to these experiences. With all the empty and pretentious conversations about gratitude that many people are currently engaging in, how do we determine if we truly have a thankful heart? Do you recognize yourself in any of these scenarios?

- You tend to focus on the imperfections in life.
- You think you'll only be happy once everything becomes perfect.
- You find fault in most things.
- You tend to only see what's missing and not what you already have.
- You believe that only bad things happen to you and the world is out to see you fail.

If any of these rings true for you, it might be time to ponder about whether you're focusing on capturing the beauty of life in its entirety. That is, valuing all the things in your life, no matter how big or small.

THE BEAUTY OF GRATITUDE

Before going into the benefits of gratitude, it's important to dispel some myths about it:

Gratitude is not a magic eraser

Embracing gratitude won't just magically solve all your problems. It certainly won't make your bad experiences disappear and wipe out all the struggles you're dealing with. Gratitude is not a spell that you say every day and hope for all your hardships to go away.

Gratitude is not about denying the existence of your emotions

Honor and acknowledge the pain you feel in whatever you're going through. Feeling grateful doesn't demand that you mask your emotions and adopt a fake thankful attitude. You will only be deceiving yourself if you do that.

The true beauty about being thankful is in knowing and accepting that things might be less than ideal but still appreciating all that is good in your life.

What you have may not be much, what you have may not be perfect, but choosing an attitude of gratitude moves us to live, to love and be thankful for the pieces of joy and hope within the imperfection.

I've had the privilege to learn this quite early on by watching my childhood friends Djamila and Daniela. Despite the weight of life's traumas and harrowing heartbreaks that they've had to endure, they've stood tall. If ever I needed a way to see how the good in life could be held onto despite overwhelming misfortune, it would be from looking at them. It's not like they have just passively resigned themselves to their fate. They have learned that bad things do happen to good people, and while they can't always get what they like, they can always change their attitude towards the situation.

While it can certainly be hard to tap into the tank of gratitude, there have been many studies pointing to the benefits that one can reap from incorporating gratitude into our daily lives. By minimizing complaints and maximizing your gratitude, you can:

Improve your well-being

Taking care of our mental and physical state is critical to our life's journey. Research has demonstrated that grateful people have better moods, less stress and more vitality. Counting your blessings can also help you sleep better and be more resilient in the face of adversity.

Take back our power

It's natural to dwell on disappointments, failures and hurtful experiences. While all the things we want have yet to materialize, if we pay close attention there are other things we can be grateful for. Gratitude helps us take our power back and deal with our feelings of inadequacy. It reminds us of what and who matters. Gratitude helps us move forward and not remain discouraged when things don't go our way.

Improve your relationships

Some people will hurt you, but others will help you. By feeling grateful and expressing appreciation to the ones who are there for you, you will bring more connectedness between them and yourself. It will also open space for more abundance in your life.

Boost your self-esteem

Being thankful is embracing and expressing gratitude. This will help you bolster your self-esteem and overall confidence. Grateful people are less prone to being envious of others.

PRACTICING GRATITUDE

If life is, according to Charles R. Swindoll, "10% of what happens to us and 90% of how we react to it," how do we go about adopting gratitude as a practice so we can react better to what happens to us? I don't think we are naturally wired to be grateful. I'm sure there are exceptions to this, but I know it took time for me to adopt a grateful attitude. I certainly don't think I was born with it. I have to intentionally practice gratitude and then it becomes part of who I am. And that's the thing with gratitude. The more you focus on the good things, the easier it will become to see all the goodness in your life.

So, a dedicated gratitude practice is fundamental if we want to make gratitude a habit and not just a once-off, spur of the moment thing. And making gratitude a habit demands commitment and patience. There are a variety of ways to adopt a practice of gratitude in your day-to-day life. The key is to ensure that you choose a practice that you like and that works for you.

If you're ready for the challenge, here are some ideas to get you started:

IN ACTION: PRACTICING GRATITUDE	
Instead of:	**Consider this:**
Struggling to make a long list of things you are grateful for.	**Find three things that you are grateful for every day.** The best way to do this is to write them down in your notebook. Remember to keep it simple.
Focusing on what you don't have yet.	**Show appreciation.** Give a compliment to somebody on a daily basis. It could be your colleague or your barista. The goal here is to put yourself aside for a minute and show appreciation to someone else.
Taking things in your life for granted.	**Imagine your life without some of the things you have.** This is a more in-depth journaling practice that we'll explore in our exercise of the day.

BETTER TIP

With

TIM FERRIS

If you haven't listened to the Tim Ferriss Show yet, you absolutely have to check it out! Hosted by the serial entrepreneur and author Tim Ferris, it's one of the most downloaded podcasts in the world. A world-class performer in his own right, Ferriss has so many ventures going on at the same time, it's hard to imagine how he manages it all. But despite his busy schedule, he still prioritizes his gratitude practice—a practice that lies at the core of his well-being. This is what he suggests doing to get your own gratitude practice started:

- First, you need to commit to setting 5 minutes aside to it in the morning and 5 minutes at night.

- Next, Ferris suggests using categories:

    - **Relationships:** think about an old relationship that was positive.

    - **Opportunity:** think about an opportunity that you have had today.

    - **Good event:** think about something good that happened yesterday or today.

    - **One thing:** think about something simple that's around you (it could be a flower, pen or notebook).

In the morning and evening pick a category and think about what you could be grateful for within that category.

A BETTER YOU

In Action

IMAGINE YOUR LIFE WITHOUT IT

How can one stop taking things for granted? How do we appreciate more of what we have and complain less about what we lack? Today's exercise is inspired by the Greater Good Science Center at the University of Berkeley. The exercise is about appreciating what you currently have by imagining your life without it. How do you do it?

- Think about a positive event in your life (personal or professional).

- Think back to that moment and all the things that happened to lead up to it.

- Now think about all the different things that could have happened and could have led to you not experiencing that positive event.

- Write down all the things and different elements that could have prevented your positive event from happening.

- Now think about what your life would have been like if that positive event hadn't occurred.

- Shift your focus back to all the rewards that this positive event brought you and appreciate that you could have missed out on these rewards.

Dedicate at least 15 minutes to this practice, one day per week. Also aim to practice this exercise at the same time every week.

EPILOGUE

"Are we there yet?" If you enjoy going on spontaneous road trips to places you've never been to before, you've probably heard—or even asked—this question at least once in your lifetime. Perhaps as you paced through the book or maybe after hitching a ride with it every page or two, the same question occasionally crossed your mind. If so, I want you to know that it's alright. In this fast-paced world, we all live to hurry along sometimes. Nevertheless, we should be reminded that to arrive *there* in a better state, fully transformed, is the ultimate goal and it takes time.

Change happens in progression and not through instant perfection.

Why do we always feel the need to rush? If we find ourselves often dissatisfied, perhaps it can be attributed to the constant asking of the wrong questions. Instead of muttering an "are we there yet?" every now and then, why not focus on the road? Whether you say it's a bumpy ride or a comforting one, merely taking the time to involve yourself in the entire experience rather than rushing to arrive at the final destination is already good enough change on its own.

The key to betterment is embracing progression rather than seeking perfection that could only yield lasting bitterness than great results.

When you expect too much of a place you have never seen before, you'll end up having greater disappointments than just enjoying the whole ride. Much as when you plant a seed, you don't check its growth on a daily basis. You trust the process, you water it despite not seeing a sprout yet. You take care of it without the least bit of certainty that it will be a beautiful, flowering plant. In life, you don't see changes right away. Small and consistent steps, on top of a fully immersive experience, lead to success and satisfaction.

There are no shortcuts and golden seeds.

Teleportation could save us a lot of time and energy because it could help us pass the obstacles in no time. There would be no more traffic congestion that could delay our journey. Surely, some magical seeds capable of growing to full maturity in a day could be handy, too. No more going to the trouble of grocery shopping, what a save! But if we chase the future and skip the process, how could we appreciate our daily victories, big or small? Whether the change we want to see is simply getting out of bed earlier or something that requires a big step towards having a career-aligned job, we need to exert effort. Every step of the way matters.

As Chadwick Boseman once said, "Take your time, but don't waste your time." Waiting for fate to take its course without doing anything is equivalent to taking our one shot at life for granted. Perhaps it's time to stop dreaming and start acting. To not waste time sitting on the gloomy and snowy sidelines waiting for an eternal sunshine. If you decide to build, grow and evolve in every season, you can reap the seeds until the end of time.

I hope you enjoyed our short but meaningful journey together. Know that it does not end here, however. The moment you made the brave choice to *own* this book, you also *owned* the philosophy of becoming braver, bolder and better. It marked the beginning of your connection with your authentic self as well as the gradual manifestation of the best life you envision. My hope is that you adopt this approach at every single turn.

A pinch of bravery, a dash of boldness and a chunk of betterment will take you further than you've ever imagined. Don't discount the small beginnings because the dots will eventually connect.

May we all heed the call from Maya Angelou to not merely survive, but to thrive, and to do so with passion, some compassion, some humor and some style.

The road is endless for the hopeful. I am rooting for you.

Keep going!

WHAT'S NEXT?

—

We are just getting started.

Go to randaadechoubou.com/bbb and enter your details to get exclusive content, bonus materials and more.

You'll automatically receive access and you'll also be added to my weekly newsletter where you will get the latest tips and strategies to help you become braver, bolder and better.

SHARING IS CARING

—

Thank you for reading Braver, Bolder, Better. If you enjoyed this book, please visit the site where you purchased it and write a brief review. I know this book can positively impact many people, and I need your help spreading the word. Nothing sells a book more than a good word of mouth, and your feedback will help other readers decide whether to read the book.

In addition to your review, I also want to know personally how this book has helped you. Email me at: Randa@randadechoubou.com. I personally read and answer all my emails.

Thank you again for reading this book and for all of your support so far. I am truly honored and grateful.

ACKNOWLEDGMENTS

—

It takes a village.

This book would not have been possible without the support, love and encouragement of so many people. From left to right, from every corner of the globe, there were amazing souls all over who believed in me, checked in and held me accountable to make sure this baby of mine would come to life. For that, I will always be grateful.

Thank you God, my father in heaven, there is no me without you.

Thank you to my parents, Makarimi and Edwige Adechoubou, my staunch supporters and loudest cheerleaders. Nothing is ever too big or small for you to encourage me to do. Thank you to Koudousse, Ahmed, Nadiath, Yacine and Rockyath, my siblings, for the unconditional love and support.

Thank you to Enyonam Adossi-Moulot, Cynthia Sole, Kekeli Kodjo, Manji Cheto, Djamila Kerim, Madje Bedou, Nina Mareini, Ladydi Mareini, Ursula Lawson, Lia Loumingou, Magali D'Almeida, Maguy Johnson—if there was a Braver, Bolder, Better club, you would be the "OGs". Thank you for continuously inspiring me to nurture my childhood dreams. One of the best things about writing this book was going down memory lane, and laughing, crying and reminiscing about all the precious times we shared. May you never forget your potential and may you always feel secure to shine your light so bright to inspire others to shine their own.

Thank you to Camille Moulot, Sadou Diallo, Lindiwe Mlalazi, Zoya Nkosi, Precious Nkosi, Daniela Amosun, Marcia Mokone, Shingai Nyagweta, Mistoura Descloux, Diana Demba-Mutondo, Willy Mutondo, Ndeye Fatou Diop, Kevin Larkai, Reon Cloete, Jake Clark and Ali Amahdar—I am so grateful to have you as inspiration. Each of you has enhanced my life in ways that I've never thought possible. Thank you for always rooting for me.

Thank you to Dr. Precious Moloi-Motsepe, Karmen Bennett, Dawn Stewart, Donna Henry, Celena Green and Pearl Darko—thank you for paving the way and inspiring me to always be the bravest, boldest and the best I can ever be. I know I am walking in the paths of giants and will forever cherish your expertise, encouragement and advice as I continue to soar higher.

Thank you to Teisha Vaughan, Adrienne Withers, Renata Lapierre, Felicity Mtetwa, Simone K. Yav and Judith Atala—I aspire to match your kindness and generosity.

Thank you to my extended family and friends: Alioun Adechoubou, Joelle Adechoubou, Joan Adechoubou, Amyr Adechoubou, Jahangir Allie, Fodé Ndiaye, Fatou Ndiaye, Maijang Mpherwane, Selaelo Ramusi, Soranna Polanco de Bravo, Aboubacar Affo, Habibou Djima, Kamaria Balkinson, Sarah Andely, Therese Toanou and family, Carlos Biaou, Patrick Nzongola, Don Teko, Douglas H. Thomas.

Kalu Mang, Kakpodjo Mahutin, Uthman Samodien, Ridhwana Shaik, Berneth Koopman, Bartholemy Sagbohan, Albine Carmen Morgean, Sarah Balemo, Sylvie Bahi Ndiaye , Aissata Madina Sylla and Pst. Nana—your support is invaluable and much appreciated.

Last and not least, thank you to my editor, Grant Murray, for helping me turn all the confusion in my head into readable and impactful stories. You rock! Thank you.

Love & Light.

Randa

RESOURCES

—

1. Sample Exercise: Meet Yourself

2. Sample Exercise: Kindness Letter

3. Shad Helmstetter's tapes are available here: https://selftalkstore.com/

4. List of Values

5. Reflected Best Self exercise here:

   https://reflectedbestselfexercise.com/

MEET YOURSELF

Yoruba. Benisese. African Writer. Storyteller. Education advocate. Business strategist. Coffee and plant lover. Fun seeker. Vintage clothes collector. All about quality, not quantity. Believer in God. Passionate about spirituality. Witty. Resourceful. Energetic. Fiercely loyal. Stubborn. Scared of the sea. Supporter of lifelong learning. Optimist. Peace seeker. All-in-or-out type of person. Loves to see others soar and thrive. Enjoys helping people reach their goals. Believes that it is never too late to be who you want to be. Sees everything in life as a miracle. Always looking for ways to improve. Bookworm. Enjoys quiet walks alone. Loves spending time with family. Loves traveling and exploring. Lived on every continent except Australia and Antarctica. Speaks Yoruba, French, English, and some Spanish. Currently learning Japanese. Believes that every day is a miracle, on an endless walk. Believes in equality of chances. Inspired by the infinite creativity in Africa. Driven to make a difference. Values freedom. Committed to a life well-lived.

LIST OF VALUES

Authenticity	Fairness	Kindness	Productivity	Significance
Acceptance	Faith	Knowledge	Professionalism	Simplicity
Achievement	Family	Lawful	Prosperity	Sincerity
Adventure	Fearless	Leadership	Purpose	Smart
Ambition	Focus	Learning	Quality	Solitude
Authority	Freedom	Liberty	Realistic	Spirituality
Balance	Friendship	Logic	Recognition	Spontaneous
Boldness	Fun	Love	Recreation	Stability
Bravery	Generosity	Loyalty	Reflective	Stewardship
Brilliance	Gratitude	Mastery	Respect	Sustainability
Community	Greatness	Maturity	Responsibility	Talent
Compassion	Growth	Meaning	Restraint	Teamwork
Competence	Happiness	Moderation	Results-oriented	Timeliness
Confidence	Harmon	Motivation	Reverence	Tolerance
Contentment	Honest	Openness	Rigor	Traditional
Courage	Hope	Optimism	Risk	Trustworthy
Curiosity	Humility	Order	Satisfaction	Uniqueness
Determination	Humor	Originality	Security	Unity
Discipline	Imagination	Passion	Self-reliance	Victory
Drive	Individuality	Patience	Selfless	Vigor
Empathy	Innovation	Peace	Sensitivity	Vision
Empower	Integrity	Persistence	Serenity	Welcoming
Energy	Joy	Power	Service	Wisdom
Ethical	Justice	Present	Sharing	Wonder

NOTES

———

CHAPTER 1: STEP UP

The Rock, "Seven Bucks Moment: Dwayne "The Rock" Johnson", December 6 2016, YouTube video, 6:00, https://www.sunnyskyz.com/happy-videos/5393/Dwayne-Johnson-Shares-His-Story-Of-Hitting-Rock-Bottom-And-How-He-Turned-His-Life-Around

CHAPTER 2: KNOW YOURSELF

Deepak Chopra, "How to Tell the Difference Between Your True Self and Your Everyday Self", *Oprah*, April 13, 2012, https://www.oprah.com/inspiration/deepak-chopra-the-difference-between-the-true-self-and-everyday-self

Tim Rettig, "The Simplest And Most Effective Exercise For Getting To Know Yourself Better", *Medium*, November 29, 2017,

https://medium.com/@rettigtim/the-simplest-and-most-effective-exercise-for-getting-to-know-yourself-better-cd34236065ee

CHAPTER 3: LOVE YOURSELF

Louise Hay, "What is Mirror Work?" *Louise Hay*, No Date, https://www.louisehay.com/what-is-mirror-work/

Tammy Mastroberte, "Learning Self Love: Louise Hay Mirror Work", *Elevated Existence*, 2016,

https://www.elevatedexistence.com/learning-self-love-louise-hay-mirror-work/

CHAPTER 4: BELIEVE YOURSELF

Shad Helmstetter, "Setting the Record Straight with Self-Talk", *Trivita*, No Date, https://www.trivita.com/setting-the-record-straight-with-self-talk/

CHAPTER 5: LIVE YOUR TRUTH

James Clear, "My 2016 Integrity Report", *James Clear*, 2016, https://jamesclear.com/2016-integrity-report

CHAPTER 6: THE APPROVAL FIX

Martha Sullivan, "How To Stop Seeking Validation From Others To Start Flourishing", *Her Way*, July 9, 2020, https://herway.net/life/how-to-stop-seeking-validation-from-others/

Zaara, "Seven Steps To Kick Your Toxic Approval-Seeking Habit", In Dr Wayne W Dyer, *Wellness, Soul Chocolate*, July 19, 2020, https://www.soulchocolate.org/seven-steps-to-kick-approval-seeking/

A Plan For Living, "Failed At Perfection? Try Self-Acceptance", *A Plan For Living*, No Date, http://www.aplanforliving.com/failed-perfection-try-self-acceptance/

Morgan Fazzini, "Our Need To Seek Approval Is Universal", *Loquitur*, December 19, 2018, https://www.theloquitur.com/our-need-to-seek-approval-is-universal/

Ottawa Therapist, "Overcoming Approval Seeking", *Clinical Practice: Individual Therapy*, March 6, 2015, https://www.ottawatherapist.ca/overcoming-approval-seeking/

Stephanie Camins, "Setting Emotional Boundaries in Relationships", *Road to Growth Counseling*, MArch 2021,

https://roadtogrowthcounseling.com/importance-boundaries-relationships/

Sharon Martin, "6 Benefits of Setting Boundaries", *Live Well With Sharon Martin*, 2016, https://livewellwithsharonmartin.com/6-benefits-of-setting-boundaries/

CHAPTER 7: THE EMOTION CODE

Nick Wignall, "4 Reasons Your Emotions Feel Out of Control", *Nick Wignall Emotional Intelligence*, July 19, 2020, https://nickwignall.com/4-reasons-your-emotions-feel-out-of-control/

Sylvia Salow, "This Is Exactly How Suppressed Emotions Rule Your Life & 5 Simple Ways to Change it", *Thrive Global*, February 10, 2016, https://medium.com/thrive-global/this-is-exactly-how-suppressed-emotions-rule-your-life-79baca98919a

Kevin Chapman, "The 3 Ingredients of All Emotions", *Psychology Today*, December 14, 2016, https://www.psychologytoday.com/us/blog/evidence-based/201612/the-3-ingredients-all-emotions

MHA, "Helpful Vs Harmful: Ways To Manage Emotions", *Mental Health America*, No Date, https://www.mhanational.org/helpful-vs-harmful-ways-manage-emotions

Claire De Boer, "How To Stop Being A Slave To Your Emotions", *Tinny Buddha*, 2015, https://tinybuddha.com/blog/how-to-stop-being-a-slave-to-your-emotions/

Gustavo Razzetti, "What Is the Best Way to Manage Your Emotions?", *Fear Less Culture*, February 25, 2019, https://liberationist.org/what-is-the-best-way-to-manage-your-emotions/

Toni Parker, "6 Steps to Mindfully Deal With Difficult Emotions", The Gottman Institute, September 28, 2016, https://www.gottman.com/blog/6stepstomindfullydealwithdifficultemotions/

Therapist Aid, "Distress Tolerance Skill", Therapist Aid L.L.C., 2015,

https://www.therapistaid.com/worksheets/dbt-distress-tolerance-skills.pdf

NOTES

CHAPTER 8: YOU BE YOU

Simi John, "Emily Blunt opens up about childhood stutter and how she overcame it", International Business times, November 30, 2018, https://www.ibtimes.co.in/emily-blunt-opens-about-childhood-stutter-how-she-overcame-it-786850#:~:text=Emily%20Blunt%20revealed%20acting%20helped%20her%20to%20overcome%20her%20childhood%20stutter.&text=During%20an%20interview%20with%20Harper's,%2C%20I%20watched%20and%20listened.%22

CHAPTER 9: LET IT GO

Alina Tugend, "Praise Is Fleeting, but Brickbats We Recall", *The New York Times*, March 23, 2012, https://www.nytimes.com/2012/03/24/your-money/why-people-remember-negative-events-more-than-positive-ones.html

Ajahn Brahm, "Have a Teflon Mind", Pinterest Quote, No Date, https://www.pinterest.com/pin/536983955568253161/

Hale Dwoskins,"How to Release Emotions using the Sedona Method Questions", *Self Help For Life*, No Date, https://selfhelpforlife.com/how-to-release-emotions-sedona-method-questions/

Everett Worthington, "REACH Forgiveness of Others", *Everett Worthington*, 2021, http://www.evworthington-forgiveness.com/reach-forgiveness-of-others

Allie Caren, "Why we often remember the bad better than the good", The Washington Post, November 1, 2018, https://www.washingtonpost.com/science/2018/11/01/why-we-often-remember-bad-better-than-good/

CHAPTER 10: FIND YOUR MAGIC

Ana Fonseca, "A BOOK REVIEW Year of Yes" by Shonda Rhimes", *The Reviting Review*, January 6, 2020, https://medium.com/the-riveting-review/year-of-yes-by-shonda-rhimes-d1726e5837b9

E. Alex Jung, "Everything We Learned About Shonda Rhimes From Her Book, Year of Yes", *Vulture Redaing Room*, November 10, 2015. https://www.vulture.com/2015/11/shonda-rhimes-year-of-yes-highlights.html

CHAPTER 11: SELF-CARE MATTERS

Tracy Kennedy, "30 Self-Care Habits for a Strong and Healthy Mind, Body and Spirit", *Life Hack*, January 12, 2021, https://www.lifehack.org/834747/self-care

CHAPTER 12: FEAR IS THE FUEL

Walk Along, "Facing Your Fears: Exposure". *Walk Along*, No Date, https://www.walkalong.ca/explore/self-help-exercises/facing-your-fears-exposure

Susan Jeffers, "The Five Truths About Fear", *Susan Jeffers*, No Date, http://www.susanjeffers.com/home/5truths.cfm

Lauren Suval , "The Positive Side of Fear", *PschyCentral*, October 30, 2018, https://psychcentral.com/blog/the-positive-side-of-fear/

Scott H. Young, "Fear is Good", *Scott H. Young*, October, 2010, https://www.scottyoung.com/blog/2010/10/14/fear-is-good/

Samovar, "How To Identify Good Fear And Kill Bad Fear On Sight", *Samovar*, No Date, https://www.samovartea.com/good-fear-bad-fear-how-to-kill-fear/

Mel Wiggins, "5 Sneaky Signs That Fear Is Running The Show In Your Life", *Mel Wiggins*, September 9, 2019,

https://www.melwiggins.com/blog/2019/9/9/5-sneaky-signs-that-fear-is-running-the-show-in-your-life-sgj67

CHAPTER 13: THE POWER OF RITUALS

Stephen Altrogge , "12 Morning and Evening Routines That Will Set Up Each Day for Success", *Zapier*, April 30, 2019, https://zapier.com/blog/daily-routines/

Steven Handel, "The Difference Between Routines vs. Rituals", *The Emotion Machine*, No Date, http://www.theemotionmachine.com/routines-vs-rituals/

Francesca Gino, Michael I. Norton , "Why Rituals Work; There are real benefits to rituals, religious or otherwise", *Scientific American*, May 14, 2013, https://www.scientificamerican.com/article/why-rituals-work/

CHAPTER 14: THE RULES TO BREAK

Abigail Johnson Hess, "4 lessons you can learn from America's first female self-made millionaire", *Make It,* February 15 2017, https://www.cnbc.com/2017/02/15/4-lessons-from-americas-first-female-self-made-millionaire.html

Guineas World Records, "First self-made millionairess", *Guineas World Records*, 2021, https://www.guinnessworldrecords.com/world-records/first-self-made-millionairess

Lisa Neumen, "Yes You DO Need To Be Breaking Rules To Get Ahead In Life", *Medium*, February 28, 2018·

https://medium.com/@lneumen/yes-you-do-need-to-be-breaking-rules-to-get-ahead-in-life-9d86f937a655

Jo Miller, "3 Rules for Rule-Breakers", *Be Leaderly*, 2021, https://beleaderly.com/3-rules-for-rule-breakers/

Josh Spector, "20 Reasons Why You Should Break The Rules", For The Interested, May 10 2017,

https://medium.com/an-idea-for-you/20-reasons-why-you-should-break-the-rules-2f13360faa74

CHAPTER 15: RISING STRONG

Laura Potier, "Soul Surfer True Story: How Much Really Happened To Bethany Hamilton", *Screen Rant*, June 04, 2020, https://screenrant.com/soul-surfer-true-story-shark-attack-bethany-hamilton/

Sports Skeeda, "Soul Surfer Bethany Hamilton shares her incredible story on Franklin Speaking podcast", *Sports Skeeda*, May 18, 2020, https://www.sportskeeda.com/mma/news-soul-surfer-bethany-hamilton-shares-incredible-story-franklin-speaking-podcast

Gunjan Upreti, "Bethany Hamilton: The One Armed Pro Surfer Will Break Your Heart, But Her Courage Will Inspire You", *Tripoto*, No Date,

https://www.tripoto.com/hawaii/trips/bethany-hamilton

Jonas Salzgeber, "Negative Visualization: The Stoic Practice to Become Mentally Stronger", *NJ Life Hacks*, December 11, 2017, https://www.njlifehacks.com/stoic-negative-visualization-become-mentally-stronger/#tab-con-3

Stoicism Definition, "How To Practice Stoic Negative Visualisation", *What Is Stoicism*, February 9, 2018, https://whatisstoicism.com/stoicism-definition/how-to-practice-stoic-negative-visualisation/

CHAPTER 16: TINY HABITS. SIGNIFICANT CHANGE

Maria Godoy, "'Tiny Habits' Are The Key To Behavioral Change", NPR, February 27, 2020, https://www.npr.org/2020/02/25/809256398/tiny-habits-are-the-key-to-behavioral-change

BJ Fogg, "You Can Succeed Just Like These People Have...", *Tiny Habits*, 2021, https://tinyhabits.com/

Brilliant Living, "What Are Habits And Why They Matter", Brilliant Living, 2019, https://www.brilliantlivinghq.com/what-are-habits-why-they-matter/

Habitica Wiki, "The Habit Loop", *Fandom*, No Date,

https://habitica.fandom.com/wiki/The_Habit_Loop

Michele Vieux, "The 3-Step Process to Turn a Bad Habit Good", *Invictus Fitness*, 2021, https://www.crossfitinvictus.com/blog/3-step-process-turn-bad-habit-good/

CHAPTER 17: GETTING THINGS DONE

Jody Michel, "How to Beat Procrastination: 14 Ways to Break the Cycle", *Jody Michel Associates*, 2021, https://www.jodymichael.com/blog/beat-procrastination/

Deprocrastination, "Chronic procrastination? What it is and how to stop it", *Deprocrastination*, No Date, https://www.deprocrastination.co/blog/chronic-procrastination-what-it-is-and-how-to-stop-it

Cari Romm, "One in Five People Are Chronic Procrastinators", The Cut, JULY 24, 2017, https://www.thecut.com/2017/07/one-in-five-people-are-chronic-procrastinators.html

Alisa Opar, "Why We Procrastinate? We Think Of Our Future Selves As Strangers", *Nautilus,* January 16, 2014,

http://nautil.us/issue/9/time/why-we-procrastinate

Chris Bailey, "5 Research-Based Strategies for Overcoming Procrastination", *Harvard Business Review*, October 04, 2017,

https://hbr.org/2017/10/5-research-based-strategies-for-overcoming-procrastination

Mel Robbins, " The five elements of the 5 second rule", *Mel Robbins,* April 25, 2018, https://melrobbins. com/five-elements-5-second-rule/

CHAPTER 18: DESTINATION GOAL

Fatihelibol, "Goal Setting Is the Only Way To Achieve Your Dreams", Fatihelibol, 15 January 2020, https://fatihelibol.com/general/goal-setting-is-the-only-way-to-achieve-your-dreams/

Daniel Dercksen, "Are You A Dreamer Or A Doer?", Writing Studio, 8 February 2016, https:// writingstudio.co.za/are-you-a-dreamer-or-a-doer/

David Allen, "Chapter 7", *A Life of Productivity*, No Date,

https://alifeofproductivity.com/resolutions/chapter7/

Alyssa Gregory, "How To Set Achievable Goals With Backward Goal Setting", *The Balance Small Business*, January 28, 2020,

https://www.thebalancesmb.com/how-to-set-achievable-goals-with-backward-goal-setting-2951823

Team Tony, "Set Smart Goals For Success", *Tony Robbins*, No Date,

https://www.tonyrobbins.com/career-business/the-6-steps-to-a-smart-goal/

CHAPTER 19: FINISH WHAT YOU START

Kendra Cherry, "How to Improve Your Self-Control", *Very Well Mind,* April 06, 2020, https://www. verywellmind.com/psychology-of-self-control-4177125

Sam Woolfe, "The Role of Self-Discipline in Mental Health", *Sam Woolfe,* August 5, 2019, https://www. samwoolfe.com/2019/08/the-role-of-discipline-in-mental-health.html

Denys Zhadanov, "Self-Discipline. Why You Need It.", *Denzhadanov,* May 23, 2020, https:// denzhadanov.com/self-discipline-why-you-need-it-bf63d838a881

The Free Press Journal, "Acceptance and Self Discipline", *The Free Press Journal*, August 5, 2012, https:// www.freepressjournal.in/ujjain/acceptance-and-self-discipline

Brian Tracy, "Embrace the 9 Rules of Self Discipline", *Cooler Insight*, July 12, 2012, https:// coolerinsights.com/2012/07/embrace-the-9-rules-of-self-discipline/

Brian Tracy, "The Practice Of Discipline", *Brian Tracy*, 2021, https://www.briantracy.com/blog/ personal-success/the-practice-of-discipline/

CHAPTER 20: BUILDING SYSTEMS FOR YOUR LIFE

Any Where, "Army Ant", *Any Where*, No date, https://www.anywhere.com/flora-fauna/invertebrates/ army-ant

TechTarget Contributor, "System", *TechTarget*, April 2005, https://searchwindowsserver.techtarget.com/definition/system

Reid, Sanders, "Operations Management: An Integrated Approach, 5th Edition", *Wiley*, October 2012, https://www.oreilly.com/library/view/operations-management-an/9781118122679/

Asian Efficiency, "How to Simplify Your Life with Systems", *Asian Efficiency*, 2021, https://www.asianefficiency.com/systems/how-to-simplify-your-life-with-systems/

https://www.habitsforwellbeing.com/tips-for-building-systems-in-to-your-current-life/

Global Learning, "What Is A World-System?", *Global Learning Cuba*, August 1, 2013, http://www.globallearning-cuba.com/blog-umlthe-view-from-the-southuml/what-is-a-world-system

CHAPTER 21: WINNING THROUGH LOSING

Benson Wong, "9 Ways To Look At Failure Differently", *Pick The Brain*, October 2, 2016, https://www.pickthebrain.com/9-ways-to-look-at-failure-differently/

Micheal Yardney, "Six Famous People Who Failed Before Succeeding", *Property Update*, March 18, 2021, https://propertyupdate.com.au/six-famous-people-who-failed-before-succeeding/

Harper West, "What Causes Fear of Failure and How to Conquer It with Self-Acceptance", *Harper West*, Dec 22, 2017, https://www.harperwest.co/what-causes-fear-of-failure-how-conquer-with-self-acceptance/

Kaung Lun, "How To Stop Fear Of Failure From Achieving Your Goals", *Journey 2 Improvement*, 2019, https://journey2improvement.com/how-to-stop-fear-of-failure-from-achieving-your-goals/

Dan Silvestre, "Set Better Personal Goals : Create a Life Worth Living (With 19 Examples)", *Dan Silvestre*, 2021, https://dansilvestre.com/personal-goals/

Motivational Speaks, "Success Story of Jack Ma, From Failures to Success", *Motivational Speaks*, January 18, 2020,

https://motivationalspeaks.com/success-story-of-jack-ma/

Srikanth AN, "Jack Ma – The Inspirational Story of Alibaba Founder", *ShoutMeLoud*, September 24, 2020, https://www.shoutmeloud.com/jack-ma-alibaba-founder.html

Patrick Buggy, "How to Conquer Your Fears and Take Action (Tim Ferriss' Fear-Setting Exercise)", *MindFul AMbition*, 2017, https://mindfulambition.net/fear-setting-tim-ferriss/

CHAPTER 22: FOCUS

Cari Nierenberg, "You can't focus on everything at once. Here's why", *NBC News*, April 21, 2011, https://www.nbcnews.com/health/body-odd/you-cant-focus-everything-once-heres-why-flna1C6437387

IVAYLO DURMONSKI, "The Ability to Focus On One Thing Will Make You Unstoppable", *Durmonski*, November, 28 2018, https://durmonski.com/self-improvement/ability-to-focus/

Couching Positive Performance, "The Importance Of Being Focused", *Couching Positive Performance*, No Date,

https://www.coachingpositiveperformance.com/the-importance-of-being-focused/

Darius Foroux, "You Can Achieve Anything If You Focus On ONE Thing", *Darius Foroux*, No Date, https://dariusforoux.com/one-thing/

The One Thing, "How to Prioritize Your Life With 2 Simple Questions", *The One Thing*, No Date, https://www.the1thing.com/blog/the-one-thing/how-to-prioritize-your-life-with-2-simple-questions/

CHAPTER 23: FIND YOUR STRENGTHS

Alice Boyes, "6 Reasons It's Hard to See Your Own Strengths", *Psychology Today*, September 10, 2018, https://www.psychologytoday.com/us/blog/in-practice/201809/6-reasons-its-hard-see-your-own-strengths

J.D. Meier, "How To Put Your Strengths to Work", *Sources of Insight*, No Date, https://sourcesofinsight.com/6-steps-for-putting-your-strengths-to-work/

Ciara Conlon, "Why Focusing on Your Strengths is the Best Philosophy", *Life Hack*, 2021, https://www.lifehack.org/articles/productivity/why-focusing-on-your-strengths-is-the-best-philosophy.html

Adam Grant, "A Better Way to Discover Your Strengths", *Huff Post*, February 2, 2013,

https://www.huffpost.com/entry/discover-your-strengths_b_3532528

Marcus Buckinghum, "Defining Strenghts", *Marcus Buckingham*, January 29, 2020, https://www.marcusbuckingham.com/defining-strengths/

CHAPTER 24: FIND YOUR WHY

Jessica Stillman, "New Harvard Research: To Be Successful, Chase Your Purpose, Not Your Passion", *Inc*, November 18, 2019, https://www.inc.com/jessica-stillman/new-harvard-research-to-be-successful-chase-your-purpose-not-your-passion.html

Aliya Alimujiang, Ashley Wiensch, Jonathan Boss, "Association Between Life Purpose and Mortality Among US Adults Older Than 50 Years", *JAMA Network*, 2019,

https://jamanetwork.com/journals/jamanetworkopen/fullarticle/2734064?utm_source=For_The_Media&utm_medium=referral&utm_campaign=ftm_links&utm_term=052419

John Templeton Foundation, "THE PSYCHOLOGY OF PURPOSE", *Templeton*, No Date, https://www.templeton.org/discoveries/the-psychology-of-purpose

Jill Suttie, "Seven Ways To Find Your Purpose In Life", *Great Good Magazine*, August 6, 2020, https://greatergood.berkeley.edu/article/item/seven_ways_to_find_your_purpose_in_life

Richard Leider, "The purpose Formula [image]", 2014, https://richardleider.com/wp-content/uploads/2014/09/ThePurposeFormula_v1.jpg

Chris Myers, "How To Find Your Ikigai And Transform Your Outlook On Life And Business", *Forbes*, February 23, 2018, https://www.forbes.com/sites/chrismyers/2018/02/23/how-to-find-your-ikigai-and-transform-your-outlook-on-life-and-business/?sh=3dad070d2ed4

CHAPTER 25: JUST LISTEN

Barry Win Bolt, "The Benefits of Being a Great Listener", *Barry Win Bolt*, August 5, 2018, https://www.barrywinbolt.com/becoming-a-great-listener/

Rachel Semigran. "6 Tips For Better Active Listening", *Goodwin College,* August 1, 2019, https://drexel.edu/goodwin/professional-studies-blog/overview/2019/August/tips-for-better-active-listening/

Skip Prichard, "The Power of Listening", *Skip Prichard*, August 12, 2016, https://www.skipprichard.com/5-ways-to-listen-better/

Julian Treasure, "5 Ways To Listen Better: TED Talk by Julian Treasure", *Suman Kher*, March 31, 2015, https://sumankher.com/2015/03/31/5-ways-to-listen-better-ted-talk-by-julian-treasure/

CHAPTER 26: YOU, INC

Robert Cialdini, "The 6 Most Persuasive Techniques You Can Use to Increase Your Influence", *Big Speak*, Septwmbwr 12, 2017,

https://www.bigspeak.com/6-persuasive-techniques-can-use-increase-influence/

Robert Cialdini, "The Principles of Persuasion Aren't Just for Business", *Influence At Work*, May 26, 2016, https://www.influenceatwork.com/principles-of-persuasion/

CHAPTER 27: PROMOTE YOURSELF

Steven Handel, "The Importance of Selling Yourself: Why Everyone Is In Sales (To A Degree)", *The Emotion Machine*, No Date, https://www.theemotionmachine.com/the-importance-of-selling-yourself/

Doug Whiteman, "The Most Hated Professions in America", *Money Wise,* January 26, 2019, https://moneywise.com/a/this-years-sleaziest-professionals

Jordan Saycell, "Warning Signs that You're Selling Yourself Short", *Medium,* October 15, 2020, https://medium.com/the-innovation/warning-signs-that-youre-selling-yourself-short-7b831be8a3a6

Renee Goyeneche, "Don't Be Shy—How To Self-Promote For Greater Success", *Forbes,* November 23, 2020, https://www.forbes.com/sites/womensmedia/2020/11/23/dont-be-shy-how-to-self-promote-for-greater-success/?sh=3feb7a284cd9

Christina Pazzanese, "Women less inclined to self-promote than men, even for a job", *The Harvard Gazette,* February 7, 2020, https://news.harvard.edu/gazette/story/2020/02/men-better-than-women-at-self-promotion-on-job-leading-to-inequities/

Christine Exley, Judd Kessler, "The gender gap in self-promotion", *Voxeu*, 23 December 2019, https://voxeu.org/article/gender-gap-self-promotion

Fordham University, "The Art Of Self-Promotion In Your Job Search", 2005, https://www. empowermentthroughopportunity.com/art%20of%20self-promotion.pdf

CHAPTER 28: YOUR NETWORK IS YOUR NETWORTH

Shelley Zalis, "Forget Networking: Relationship Building Is The Best Career Shortcut", *Forbes,* February 23, 2018, https://www.forbes.com/sites/shelleyzalis/2018/02/23/forget-networking-relationship-building-is-the-best-career-shortcut/?sh=7d4893afbf7d

Zet Gallery, "Never Eat Alone" – 10 tips for a successful professional career, *Zet Gallery*, June 2, 2020, http://zet.gallery/blog/en/never-eat-alone-10-tips-for-successful-professional-career/

CHAPTER 29: YOU 2.0

Courtney Connely, "How a career change at 32 led Ava DuVernay to become the first black woman to direct a $100 million film", *Make It,* March 10 2018, https://www.cnbc.com/2018/03/09/a-career-change-at-32-led-ava-duvernay-to-directing-blockbusters.html

Shipra Harbola Gupta, "Tribeca: Ava DuVernay's 8 Tips to Filmmakers On How to Stay in Control", *Indie Wire,* Apr 23, 2015, https://www.indiewire.com/2015/04/tribeca-ava-duvernays-8-tips-to-filmmakers-on-how-to-stay-in-control-62755/

National Wellness Institute, "THE SIX DIMENSIONS OF WELLNESS", *National Wellness Institute,* 2020, https://nationalwellness.org/resources/six-dimensions-of-wellness/

CHAPTER 30: GRATITUDE

Greater Good, "What Is Gratitude?", *Greater Good Magazine,* No Date, https://greatergood.berkeley.edu/topic/gratitude/definition#why_practice

Tim Ferriss, "Don't Like Meditation? Try Gratitude Training. (Plus: Follow-Up To "Testing Friends" Firestorm)", *Tim,* November 19, 2007, https://tim.blog/2007/11/19/dont-like-meditation-try-gratitude-training-plus-follow-up-to-testing-friends-firestorm/

Greater Good, "What Is Gratitude?", *Greater Good Magazine,* No Date, https://greatergood.berkeley.edu/topic/gratitude/definition#why_practice

Catherine Robertson, "How Gratitude Can Change Your Life", *Rickanson,* 2021, https://www.rickhanson.net/how-gratitude-can-change-your-life/

INDEX

A

abandoned 1, 2, 3

ABUNDANCE 88

accountability 25, 60, 120

accustomed 105, 181, 280

acknowledge 8, 77, 234, 256, 298

actionable value 61

action-packed 7

admiration 64

adrenaline 291

adventure 7, 56, 104

affirmations 38, 41, 43, 138

Albert Einstein 107, 203

ambitions 2, 33, 181, 281

ammunition 96

anger 70, 80, 95, 97, 100, 153

anxiety 67, 76, 107, 224

appreciate 217, 303, 305

APPROVAL FIX 63, 316

approval-seeking behavior 68, 69

arrogant 269, 272

Art of Gratitude 16

ART OF PERSUASION 262

Ava Duvernay 16, 293

awareness 3, 32, 33, 135, 225, 234, 292, 294

B

bad character 57

bad memories 94

Be curious 283

Behavioral Change 319

Believe in Yourself 9

Benjamin Franklin 11, 139

Bethany Hamilton 12, 157, 319

betterment 4, 209, 225, 304, 306

bite-sized tweets 252

bitterness 304

bolder 7, 10, 11, 91, 306, 307

Boundaries 70, 316

brainstorming 61

BRAVER i, ii, 8, 17, 24, 25, 35, 36, 43, 44, 51, 53, 60, 61, 69, 70, 80, 90, 91, 99, 100, 109, 110

Brian Tracy 13, 196, 320

C

challenges 3, 7, 74, 148, 153, 185, 193

chastised 66

clarity 33, 35, 57, 91, 203, 231

comfort zone 4, 103, 105, 106, 107, 108, 109, 110, 143, 154, 192, 246, 291

commitment 8, 17, 41, 67, 99, 107, 181, 182, 190, 254, 264, 273, 300

companion 8, 43

competition 10, 282

compromising 58

concentrate 14

confidence 33, 38, 47, 83, 134, 136, 153, 154, 235, 254, 271, 274, 300

Congratulations 4

conquer 11, 154, 321

consistency 8, 41, 135, 155, 164, 226, 264

convince 15, 56, 69, 136, 144, 170, 261, 263, 264, 265

creativity 11

criticism 215

crusader 39

D

Dangerous 76

David Allen 13, 186, 192, 320

dead-end relationship 23

debates 7

debilitating 90, 126

Deepak Chopra 8, 35, 315

Deeper connections 254

dehumanizing 143

DESTINATION GOAL 320

devastating 1, 2, 3, 97, 157, 220

directionless 1, 3

disappointment 100, 182

discomfort 31, 58, 173, 191, 193, 260

disheveled 203

disparagingly 95

distractions 14, 196, 225, 228, 255

Dr. BJ Fogg 12, 166

Dr. Cialdini 15

Dwayne "The Rock" 8, 24, 315

E

education 220, 325

embarked 1, 293

Emily Blunt 10, 90, 317

EMOTIONAL BALANCE 77

Emotion Code 10

empower 50

encounter 8, 21, 74, 193, 216

entertain 11, 20, 21, 48, 87

entrepreneurship 48, 148

epiphany 246

eradicate 7, 49, 100, 274

Everett Worthington 10, 99, 317

exhaust 2

F

failed experiment 56

Failing Forward 14

Failure 14, 213, 216, 217, 219, 321

fault-finding 124

Fear Is The Fuel 11

Fear of rejection 215

Fear of shame 214

feigning ignorance 30

fertile soil 11

flagship projects 190

forbid 64

Forgiveness 93, 95, 96, 97, 98, 99, 100, 317

Foundation 322

frustrations 124

G

Gain Mastery 226

Gary W. Keller 14

generous 57, 285

glory 2, 236

Gottman Institute 10, 80, 316

Gratefulness 16

gratitude 16, 89, 209, 297, 298, 299, 300, 302, 324

greatness 7, 157

groundbreaking 12, 14, 109, 176, 229

growth 10, 16, 39, 91, 107, 143, 145, 153, 216, 238, 239, 290, 305

grudge 94

guilt 194

H

harboring resentment 98

headquarters 56

healthy habits 5

hear 90, 105, 152, 190, 201, 212, 213, 215, 252, 253, 260

horrified 90

I

Imposter syndrome 270

Improved confidence 254

Integrity Report 9, 60, 315

idiots 105

illuminating 3

imperfections 44, 297

impression 67, 284

impulsive shopping 11

incredible tips 16

inspirational speaker 86

inspirational stuff 8

inspire 3, 12, 16, 86, 96, 203, 217, 250, 309, 325, 332

interject 64, 252

J

Jack Ma 14, 220, 321

James Clear 9, 60, 202, 315

Jane Taylor 13, 205

Jay Papasan 14, 229

Julian Treasure 15, 256, 323

K

Keith Ferrazzi 16, 285

kindness letter 44

Know yourself 274

L

lack of growth 290

landscapes 7

Less stress 226

LET IT GO 93, 103, 317

LIVE YOUR TRUTH 315

listless 290

Loss aversion 215

Louise Hay 9, 43, 315

Love and war 38

M

Madam CJ Walker 12

Marcus Buckingham 14, 234, 238, 239

Marrakesh 20

Maslow's hierarchy 65

Mel Robbins 12, 176, 320

memories 15, 94, 95, 180

mentally strong 152, 154, 155, 217

Mental toughness 192

MINDSET 49, 88

millionaire 12, 148, 318

mind-boggling moments 20

mindsets 7

miraculously 22, 244, 268

misfortune 2, 298

mission 88, 244, 250, 325

misunderstanding 255, 262

motivational speaker 21, 46, 69, 176

mummies' tombs 242

N

natural talents 192, 227

negative thoughts 67, 95, 138, 156

Negative visualization 158

O

obstacles 7, 126, 151, 305

operating system 13

opportunities 4, 15, 33, 67, 95, 106, 126, 143, 153, 170, 191, 227, 239, 255, 271, 282, 290

overindulging 77, 116

P

Peggy Klaus 16, 275

people's fantasies 30

people's priorities 29, 34, 225

perception of joy 31

perfection 64, 86, 126, 304, 316

perfectionism 64

PERSUADING 261, 263

philosophy 9, 127, 130, 201, 212, 306, 322

physical fatigue 67

physical strength 155

poison 97

poisonously selfless 2

politeness 9

potential experiences 1

power of repetition 9

Power of Rituals 11

predictable 56, 106, 107, 135, 236

premature death 77

pretentious conversations 297

Principles of Persuasion 15, 323

procrastinate 67, 170, 171, 172, 173, 214, 235, 319

productivity 11, 186, 322

professional success 58

professional wrestler 24

PROMOTE YOURSELF 323

psychological principle 47

psychologists 85, 125

R

Reciprocity 264

redundant 153

relationships 57, 65, 74, 91, 197, 230, 254, 274, 281, 282, 284, 285, 299, 316

relinquishing 107

resentment 70, 95, 98, 271

resilience 24, 154, 217, 220

restrictive life 193

RISING STRONG 151, 159, 169, 179, 189, 199, 211, 319

Richard Leider 15, 247, 322

ridiculousness 20

road trip 7

Rules to Break 12

ruminate 74, 96

S

sabbatical 144, 246

sabotage 67

satisfaction 249, 305

Savoring 256

Scarcity 264

self-abandonment 2, 4

self-acceptance 9, 30, 316, 321

self-actualization 4

self-advocacy 209, 271, 272, 273

Self-care 11, 113, 115, 117, 228

self-criticizing 9

self-defeating 171

self-discipline 189, 190, 191, 192, 193, 194, 195, 196, 197, 320

self-esteem 32, 48, 65, 84, 174, 194, 254, 300

self-improvement 14, 86, 321

self-promotion 15, 269, 270, 271, 273, 275, 323

SELF-REINVENTION 289, 291

semi-coherent 20

Shad Helmstetter 9, 51, 312, 315

shame 97, 194, 214, 281

Shonda Rhimes 10, 109, 110, 317

smashing your goals 49

snorkeling activity 104

socializing 192

Social proof 264

sparkling water 28

spiritual 49, 294

strange creatures 75

strategist 46, 200

stumble 14, 216

stuttering 10, 90

success 14, 50, 58, 60, 88, 90, 107, 148, 153, 154,
164, 166, 172, 181, 182, 183, 185, 189, 191,
193, 196, 213, 215, 216, 218, 219, 226, 235,
245, 261, 271, 273, 281, 285, 293, 305, 320,
321, 323

successful entrepreneurs 136

supernatural 46

surrender 162

Susan Jeffers 11, 130, 317

T

Tedious 135

Tim Ferris 16, 221, 302

transformation 7, 158, 291

trap 268

trust yourself 68

U

unapologetically 67

uncontrollable waves 74

unhealthy 47, 67, 70, 76, 77, 86, 97, 124, 224

Uninspired 290

unique abilities 86

Upbringing 269

W

Wayne Dyer 9, 69

weakness 234

Y

yellow signage 114

ABOUT THE AUTHOR

———

R anda is an optimist working at the nexus of education, business and philanthropy. She holds a master's in business administration (MBA) from the University of Cape Town (UCT) and a BPhil in political science from Northwestern University. An author and advocate on a mission, Randa strives to tell rich narratives that inspire others to proudly live their truth. When she's not writing in her favorite coffee shop, Randa is exploring or daydreaming about her next travel destination. Learn more about Randa, and check out her current projects at www.randaadechoubou.com.

IYA-OLOKA
PUBLISHING.CO

Iya-oloka is an independently owned publisher, specializing in books that tell relevant, uplifting, and powerful stories.

At Iya-oloka, we are proud to produce and promote the highest-quality books that we hope will inspire generations of readers to bring about positive changes in their own lives and share that positivity with those around them.

Visit us at:

www.Iya-oloka.com

www.ingramcontent.com/pod-product-compliance
Lightning Source LLC
Chambersburg PA
CBHW021952090426
42811CB00041B/2410/J